A MAN FOR ALL SEASONS

A MAN
FOR ALL SEASONS

A Play in Two Acts

———————⋙⋘———————

by Robert Bolt

RANDOM HOUSE • NEW YORK

SIR THOMAS MORE

More is a man of an angel's wit and singular learning; I know not his fellow. For where is the man of that gentleness, lowliness, and affability? And as time requireth a man of marvellous mirth and pastimes; and sometimes of as sad gravity: a man for all seasons.

Robert Whittinton

He was the person of the greatest virtue these islands ever produced.

Samuel Johnson

The bit of English history which is the background to this play is pretty well known. Henry VIII, who started with everything and squandered it all, who had the physical and mental fortitude to endure a lifetime of gratified greeds, the monstrous baby whom none dared gainsay, is one of the most popular figures in the whole procession. We recognize in him an archetype, one of the champions of our baser nature, and are in him vicariously indulged.

Against him stood the whole edifice of medieval religion, founded on piety, but by then as moneyed, elaborate, heaped high and inflexible as those abbey churches which Henry brought down with such a satisfying and disgraceful crash.

The collision came about like this: While yet a Prince, Henry did not expect to become a King, for he had an elder brother, Arthur. A marriage was made between this Arthur and a Spanish Princess, Catherine, but Arthur presently died. The Royal Houses of Spain and England wished to repair the connection, and the obvious way to do it was to marry the young widow to Henry, now heir in Arthur's place. But Spain and England were Christian monarchies and Christian law forbade a man to marry his brother's widow.

To be a Christian was to be a Churchman and there was only one Church (though plagued with many heresies) and the Pope was its head. At the request of Christian Spain and Christian England the Pope dispensed with the Christian law forbidding a man to marry his brother's widow, and when in due course Prince Henry ascended the English throne as Henry VIII, Catherine was his Queen.

For some years the marriage was successful; they respected

and liked one another, and Henry took his pleasures elsewhere but lightly. However, at length he wished to divorce her.

The motives for such a wish are presumably as confused, inaccessible and helpless in a King as any other man, but here are three which make sense: Catherine had grown increasingly plain and intensely religious; Henry had fallen in love with Anne Boleyn; the Spanish alliance had become unpopular. None of these absolutely necessitated a divorce but there was a fourth that did. Catherine had not been able to provide Henry with a male child and was now presumed barren. There was a daughter, but competent statesmen were unanimous that a Queen on the throne of England was unthinkable. Anne and Henry were confident that between them they could produce a son; but if that son was to be Henry's heir, Anne would have to be Henry's wife.

The Pope was once again approached, this time by England only, and asked to declare the marriage with Catherine null, on the grounds that it contravened the Christian law which forbade marriage with a brother's widow. But England's insistence that the marriage had been null was now balanced by Spain's insistence that it hadn't. And at that moment Spain was well placed to influence the Pope's deliberations; Rome, where the Pope lived, had been very thoroughly sacked and occupied by Spanish troops. In addition one imagines a natural disinclination on the part of the Pope to have his powers turned on and off like a tap. At all events, after much ceremonious prevarication, while Henry waited with a rising temper, it became clear that so far as the Pope was concerned, the marriage with Catherine would stand.

To the ferment of a lover and the anxieties of a sovereign Henry now added a bad conscience; and a serious matter it was, for him and those about him.

The Bible, he found, was perfectly clear on such marriages as he had made with Catherine; they were forbidden. And the threatened penalty was exactly what had befallen him, the failure of male heirs. He was in a state of sin. He had been thrust into a state of sin by his father with the active help of the Pope. And the Pope now proposed to keep him in a state of sin. The man who would do that, it began to seem to Henry, had small claim to being the Vicar of God.

And indeed, on looking into the thing really closely, Henry found—what various voices had urged for centuries off and on —that the supposed Pope was no more than an ordinary bishop, the Bishop of Rome. This made everything clear and everything possible. If the Pope was not a Pope at all but merely a bishop among bishops, then his special powers as Pope did not exist. In particular, of course, he had no power to dispense with God's rulings as revealed in Leviticus 18, but equally important, he had no power to appoint other bishops; and here an ancient quarrel stirred.

For if the Pope had not the power to appoint bishops, then who did have, if not the King himself—King by the Grace of God? Henry's ancestors, all those other Henries, had been absolutely right; the Bishops of Rome, without a shadow of legality, had succeeded over the centuries in setting up a rival reign within the reign, a sort of long-drawn usurpation. The very idea of it used to throw him into terrible rages. It should go on no longer.

He looked about for a good bishop to appoint to Canterbury, a bishop with no ambitions to modify God's ruling on deceased brothers' wives, yet sufficiently spirited to grant a divorce to his sovereign without consulting the Bishop of Rome. The man was to hand in Thomas Cranmer; Catherine was divorced,

PREFACE

Anne married, and the Established Church of England was off on its singular way.

That, very roughly indeed, is the political, or theological, or politico-theological background to the play. But what of the social, or economic, or socio-economic, which we now think more important?

The economy was very progressive, the religion was very reactionary. We say therefore that the collision was inevitable, setting Henry aside as a colorful accident. With Henry presumably we set aside as accidents Catherine and Wolsey and Anne and More and Cranmer and Cromwell and the Lord Mayor of London and the man who cleaned his windows; setting indeed everyone aside as an accident, we say that the collision was inevitable. But that, on reflection, seems only to repeat that it happened. What is of interest is the way it happened, the way it was lived. For lived such collisions are. "Religion" and "economy" are abstractions which describe the way men live. Because men work we may speak of an economy, not the other way round. Because men worship we may speak of a religion, not the other way round. And when an economy collides with a religion it is living men who collide, nothing else (they collide with one another and within themselves).

Perhaps few people would disagree with that, put like that, and in theory. But in practice our theoreticians seem more and more to work the other way round, to derive the worker *from* his economy, the thinker *from* his culture, and we to derive even ourselves from our society and our location in it. When we ask ourselves "What am I?" we may answer "I am a Man" but are conscious that it's a silly answer because we don't know what kind of thing that might be; and feeling the answer silly we feel it's probably a silly question. We can't help asking it, however, for natural curiosity makes us ask it all the time of

everyone else, and it would seem artificial to make ourselves
the sole exception, would indeed envelop the mental image of
our self in a unique silence and thus raise the question in a
particularly disturbing way. So we answer of ourselves as we
should of any other: "This man here is a qualified surveyor,
employed but with a view to partnership; this car he is driving
has six cylinders and is almost new; he's doing all right; his
opinions . . ." and so on, describing ourselves to ourselves in
terms more appropriate to somebody seen through a window.
We think of ourselves in the Third Person.

To put it another way, more briefly; we no longer have, as
past societies have had, any picture of individual Man (Stoic
Philosopher, Christian Religious, Rational Gentleman) by
which to recognize ourselves and against which to measure ourselves; we are anything. But if anything, then nothing, and it
is not everyone who can live with that, though it is our true
present position. Hence our willingness to locate ourselves from
something that is certainly larger than ourselves, the society
that contains us.

But society can only have as much idea as we have what we
are about, for it has only our brains to think with. And the
individual who tries to plot his position by reference to our
society finds no fixed points, but only the vaunted absence of
them, "freedom" and "opportunity"; freedom for what, opportunity to do what, is nowhere indicated. The only positive he
is given is "get and spend" ("get and spend—if you can" from
the Right, "get and spend—you deserve it" from the Left) and
he did not need society to tell him that. In other words we are
thrown back by our society upon ourselves at our lowest, that
is at our least satisfactory to ourselves. Which of course sends
us flying back to society with all the force of rebound.

Socially, we fly from the idea of an individual to the professional describers, the classifiers, the men with the categories and a quick ear for the latest subdivision, who flourish among us like priests. Individually, we do what we can to describe and classify ourselves and so assure ourselves that from the outside at least we do have a definite outline. Both socially and individually it is with us as it is with our cities—an accelerating flight to the periphery, leaving a center which is empty when the hours of business are over.

That is an ambitious style of thinking, and pride cometh before a fall, but it was with some such ideas in mind that I started on this play. Or else they developed as I wrote it. Or else I have developed them in defense of it now that it is written. It is not easy to know what a play is "about" until it is finished, and by then what it is "about" is incorporated in it irreversibly and is no more to be separated from it than the shape of a statue is to be separated from the marble. Writing a play is thinking, not thinking about thinking; more like a dream than a scheme—except that it lasts six months or more, and that one is responsible for it.

At any rate, Thomas More, as I wrote about him, became for me a man with an adamantine sense of his own self. He knew where he began and left off, what area of himself he could yield to the encroachments of his enemies, and what to the encroachments of those he loved. It was a substantial area in both cases, for he had a proper sense of fear and was a busy lover. Since he was a clever man and a great lawyer he was able to retire from those areas in wonderfully good order, but at length he was asked to retreat from that final area where he located his self. And there this supple, humorous, unassuming and sophisticated person set like metal, was overtaken by an absolutely primitive rigor, and could no more be budged than a cliff.

xii

PREFACE

This account of him developed as I wrote: what first attracted me was a person who could not be accused of any incapacity for life, who indeed seized life in great variety and almost greedy quantities, who nevertheless found something in himself without which life was valueless and when that was denied him was able to grasp his death. For there can be no doubt, given the circumstances, that he did it himself. If, on any day up to that of his execution, he had been willing to give public approval to Henry's marriage with Anne Boleyn, he could have gone on living. Of course the marriage was associated with other things—the attack on the abbeys, the whole Reformation policy—to which More was violently opposed, but I think he could have found his way round those; he showed every sign of doing so. Unfortunately his approval of the marriage was asked for in a form that required him to state that he believed what he didn't believe, and required him to state it on oath.

This brings me to something for which I feel the need to explain, perhaps apologize. More was a very orthodox Catholic and for him an oath was something perfectly specific; it was an invitation to God, an invitation God would not refuse, to act as a witness, and to judge; the consequence of perjury was damnation, for More another perfectly specific concept. So for More the issue was simple (though remembering the outcome it can hardly have been easy). But I am not a Catholic nor even in the meaningful sense of the word a Christian. So by what right do I appropriate a Christian saint to my purposes? Or to put it the other way, why do I take as my hero a man who brings about his own death because he can't put his hand on an old black book and tell an ordinary lie?

For this reason: A man takes an oath only when he wants to commit himself quite exceptionally to the statement, when he wants to make an identity between the truth of it and his own virtue; he offers himself as a guarantee. And it works. There is a special kind of shrug for a perjurer; we feel that the man has no self to commit, no guarantee to offer. Of course it's much less effective now that for most of us the actual words of the oath are not much more than impressive mumbo-jumbo than it was when they made obvious sense; we would prefer most men to guarantee their statements with, say, cash rather than with themselves. We feel—we know—the self to be an equivocal commodity. There are fewer and fewer things which, as they say, we "cannot bring ourselves" to do. We can find almost no limits for ourselves other than the physical, which, being physical, are not optional. Perhaps this is why we have fallen back so widely on physical torture as a means of bringing pressure to bear on one another. But though few of us have anything in ourselves like an immortal soul which we regard as absolutely inviolable, yet most of us still feel something which we should prefer, on the whole, not to violate. Most men feel when they swear an oath (the marriage vow for example) that they have invested something. And from this it's possible to guess what an oath must be to a man for whom it is not merely a time-honored and understood ritual but also a definite contract. It may be that a clear sense of the self can *only* crystallize round something transcendental in which case, our prospects look poor, for we are rightly committed to the rational. I think the paramount gift our thinkers, artists, and for all I know, our men of science, should labor to get for us is a sense of selfhood without resort to magic. Albert Camus is a writer I admire in this connection.

Anyway, the above must serve as my explanation and apology for treating Thomas More, a Christian saint, as a hero of selfhood.

PREFACE

Another thing that attracted me to this amazing man was his splendid social adjustment. So far from being one of society's sore teeth he was, like the hero of Camus' *La Chute*, almost indecently successful. He was respectably, not nobly, born, in the merchant class, the progressive class of the epoch, distinguished himself first as a scholar, then as a lawyer, was made an Ambassador, finally Lord Chancellor. A visitors' book at his house in Chelsea would have looked like a sixteenth-century *Who's Who*: Holbein, Erasmus, Colet, everybody. He corresponded with the greatest minds in Europe as the representative and acknowledged champion of the New Learning in England. He was a friend of the King, who would send for More when his social appetites took a turn in that direction and once walked round the Chelsea garden with his arm round More's neck. ("If my head would win him a castle in France, it should not fail to fall," said More.) He adored and was adored by his own large family. He parted with more than most men when he parted with his life, for he accepted and enjoyed his social context.

One sees that there is no necessary contradiction here; it is society after all which proffers an oath and with it the opportunity for perjury. But why did a man so utterly absorbed in his society, at one particular point disastrously part company from it? How indeed was it possible—unless there was some sudden aberration? But that explanation won't do, because he continued to the end to make familiar and confident use of society's weapons, tact, favor, and, above all, the letter of the law.

For More again the answer to this question would be perfectly simple (though again not easy); the English Kingdom, his immediate society, was subservient to the larger society of the Church of Christ, founded by Christ, extending over Past and Future, ruled from Heaven. There are still some for whom that is perfectly simple, but for most it can only be a metaphor. I took it as a metaphor for that larger context which we all inhabit, the terrifying cosmos. Terrifying because no laws, no sanctions, no *mores* obtain there; it is either empty or occupied by God and Devil nakedly at war. The sensible man will seek to live his life without dealings with this larger environment, treating it as a fine spectacle on a clear night, or a subject for innocent curiosity. At the most he will allow himself an agreeable *frisson* when he contemplates his own relation to the cosmos, but he will not try to live in it; he will gratefully accept the shelter of his society. This was certainly More's intention.

If "society" is the name we give to human behavior when it is patterned and orderly, then the Law (extending from empirical traffic regulations, through the mutating laws of property, and on to the great taboos like incest and patricide) is the very pattern of society. More's trust in the law was his trust in his society; his desperate sheltering beneath the forms of the law was his determination to remain within the shelter of society. Cromwell's contemptuous shattering of the forms of law by an unconcealed act of perjury showed how fragile for any individual is that shelter. Legal or illegal had no further meaning, the social references had been removed. More was offered, to be sure, the chance of slipping back into the society which had thrust him out into the warring cosmos, but even in that solitude he found himself able to repeat, or continue, the decision he had made while he still enjoyed the common shelter.

I see that I have used a lot of metaphors. I know no other way to treat this subject. In the play I used for this theme a poetic image. As a figure for the superhuman context I took the largest, most alien, least formulated thing I know, the sea and water. The references to ships, rivers, currents, tides, navigation, and so on, are all used for this purpose. Society by contrast figures as dry land. I set out with no very well-formed idea of the kind of play it was to be, except that it was not to be naturalistic. The possibility of using imagery, that is of using metaphors not decoratively but with an intention, was a side effect of that. It's a very far from new idea, of course. Whether it worked I rather doubt. Certainly no one noticed. But I comfort myself with the thought that it's the nature of imagery to work, in performance at any rate, unconsciously. But if, as I think, a play is more like a poem than a straight narration, still less a demonstration or lecture, then imagery ought to be important. It's perhaps necessary to add that by a poem I mean something tough and precise, not something dreamy. As Brecht said, beauty and form of language are a primary alienation device. I was guaranteed some beauty and form by incorporating passages from Sir Thomas More himself. For the rest my concern was to match with these as best I could so that the theft should not be too obvious.

In two previous plays, *Flowering Cherry* and *The Tiger and the Horse*, I had tried, but with fatal timidity, to handle contemporaries in a style that should make them larger than life; in the first mainly by music and mechanical effects, in the second mainly by making the characters unnaturally articulate and unnaturally aware of what they "stood for." Inevitably these plays looked like what they most resembled, orthodox fourth-wall dramas with puzzling, uncomfortable, and, if you are uncharitable, pretentious overtones. So for this one I took a historical setting in the hope that the distance of years would give me Dutch courage, and enable me to treat my characters in a properly heroic, properly theatrical manner.

PREFACE

The style I eventually used was a bastardized version of the one most recently associated with Bertolt Brecht. This is not the place to discuss that style at any length, but it does seem to me that the style practiced by Brecht differs from the style taught by Brecht, or taught to us by his disciples. Perhaps they are more Royalist than the King. Or perhaps there was something daemonic in Brecht the artist which could not submit to Brecht the teacher. That would explain why in the *Chalk Circle,* which is to demonstrate that goodness is a terrible temptation, goodness triumphs very pleasantly. And why in *Mother Courage,* which is to demonstrate the unheroic nature of war, the climax is an act of heroism which Rider Haggard might have balked at. And why in *Galileo,* which is to demonstrate the social and objective value of scientific knowledge, Galileo, congratulated on saving his skin so as to augment that knowledge, is made to deny its value on the grounds that he defaulted at the moment when what the world needed was for one man to be true to himself. I am inclined to think that it is simply that Brecht was a very fine artist, and that life is complicated and ambivalent. At all events I agree with Eric Bentley that the proper effect of alienation is to enable the audience *reculer pour mieux sauter,* to deepen, not to terminate, their involvement in the play.

Simply to slap your audience in the face satisfies an austere and puritanical streak which runs in many of his disciples and sometimes, detrimentally I think, in Brecht himself. But it is a dangerous game to play. It has the effect of shock because it is unexpected. But it is unexpected only because it flies in the face of a thoroughly established convention (a convention which goes far beyond naturalism; briefly, the convention that the actors are there as actors, not as themselves). Each time it is done it is a little less unexpected, so that a bigger and bigger dosage will be needed to produce the same effect. If it were continued indefinitely it would finally not be unexpected at all. The theatrical convention would then have been entirely dissipated and we should have in the theatre a situation with one person, who used to be an actor, desperately trying to engage the attention—by rude gestures, loud noises, indecent exposure, fireworks, anything—of other persons, who used to be the audience. As this point was approached some very lively evenings might be expected, but the depth and subtlety of the notions which can be communicated by such methods may be doubted. When we use alienation methods just for kicks, we in the theatre are sawing through the branch on which we are sitting.

I tried then for a "bold and beautiful verbal architecture," a story rather than a plot, and overtly theatrical means of switching from one locale to another. I also used the most notorious of the alienation devices, an actor who addresses the audience and comments on the action. But I had him address the audience in character, that is, from within the play.

He is intended to draw the audience into the play, not thrust them off it. In this respect he largely fails, and for a reason I had not foreseen. He is called "The Common Man" (just as there is a character called "The King") and the word "common" was intended primarily to indicate "that which is common to us all." But he was taken instead as a portrayal of that mythical beast, The Man in the Street. This in itself was not so bad; after all he was intended to be something with which everyone would be able to identify. But once he was identified as common in that sense, my character was by one party accepted as a properly belittling account of that vulgar person, and by another party bitterly resented on his behalf. (Myself I had meant him to be attractive, and his

PREFACE

philosophy impregnable.) What both these parties had in common—if I may use the word—is that they thought of him as
somebody else. Wherever he might have been, this Common
Man, he was certainly not in the theatre. He is harder to
find than a unicorn. But I must modify that. He was not in
the stalls, among his fashionable detractors and defenders. But
in the laughter this character drew down from the gallery,
that laughter which is the most heartening sound our Theatre
knows, I thought I heard once or twice a rueful note of rec-
ognition.

ROBERT BOLT

September, 1960

A MAN FOR ALL SEASONS *was first presented by Robert White-head and Roger L. Stevens at the ANTA Theatre, New York City, New York, on November 22, 1961, with the following cast:*

(IN ORDER OF APPEARANCE)

THE COMMON MAN	George Rose
SIR THOMAS MORE	Paul Scofield
RICHARD RICH	William Redfield
THE DUKE OF NORFOLK	Albert Dekker
ALICE MORE	Carol Goodner
MARGARET MORE	Olga Bellin
CARDINAL WOLSEY	Jack Creley
THOMAS CROMWELL	Thomas Gomez
SIGÑOR CHAPUYS, the Spanish Ambassador	David J. Stewart
HIS ATTENDANT	John Colenback
WILLIAM ROPER	Peter Brandon
KING HENRY VIII	Keith Baxter
THE WOMAN	Sarah Burton
CRANMER, Archbishop of Canterbury	Lester Rawlins

Directed by NOEL WILLMAN
Settings and costumes by MOTLEY
Lighting by PAUL MORRISON
Produced by arrangement with H. M. TENNENT LTD.

People In The Play

THE COMMON MAN: Late middle age. He wears from head to foot black tights which delineate his pot-bellied figure. His face is crafty, loosely benevolent, its best expression that of base humor.

SIR THOMAS MORE: Late forties. Pale, middle-sized, not robust. But the life of the mind in him is so abundant and debonair that it illuminates the body. His movements are open and swift but never wild, having a natural moderation. The face is intellectual and quickly delighted, the norm to which it returns serious and compassionate. Only in moments of high crisis does it become ascetic—though then freezingly.

RICHARD RICH: Early thirties. A good body unexercised. A studious unhappy face lit by the fire of banked-down appetite. He is an academic hounded by self-doubt to be in the world of affairs and longing to be rescued from himself.

DUKE OF NORFOLK: Late forties. Heavy, active, a sportsman and soldier held together by rigid adherence to the minimal code of conventional duty. Attractively aware of his moral and intellectual insignificance, but also a great nobleman, untouchably convinced that his acts and ideas are important because they are his.

ALICE MORE: Late forties. Born into the merchant class, now a great lady; she is absurd at a distance, impressive close to. Overdressed, coarsely fashioned, she worships society; brave, hot-hearted, she worships her husband. In consequence, troubled by and defiant towards both.

MARGARET MORE: Middle twenties. A beautiful girl of ardent moral fineness; she both suffers and shelters behind a reserved stillness which it is her father's care to mitigate.

CARDINAL WOLSEY: Old. A big decayed body in scarlet. An almost megalomaniac ambition unhappily matched by an excelling intellect, he now inhabits a lonely den of self-indulgence and contempt.

THOMAS CROMWELL: Late thirties. Subtle and serious; the face expressing not inner tension but the tremendous outgoing will of the renaissance. A self-conceit that can cradle gross crimes in the name of effective action. In short, an intellectual bully.

CHAPUYS: Sixties. A professional diplomat and lay ecclesiastic dressed in black. Much on his dignity as a man of the world, he in fact trots happily along a mental footpath as narrow as a peasant's.

CHAPUYS' ATTENDANT: An apprentice diplomat of good family.

WILLIAM ROPER: Early thirties; a stiff body and an immobile face. Little imagination, moderate brain, but an all-consuming rectitude which is his cross, his solace, and his hobby.

THE KING: Not the Holbein Henry, but a much younger man, clean-shaven, bright-eyed, graceful and athletic. The Golden Hope of the New Learning throughout Europe. Only the levity with which he handles his absolute power foreshadows his future corruption.

A WOMAN: Middle fifties. Self-opinionated, self-righteous, selfish, indignant.

CRANMER: Late forties. Sharp-minded, sharp-faced. He treats the Church as a job of administration, and theology as a set of devices, for he lacks personal religiosity.

THE SET is the same throughout but capable of varied lightings, as indicated. Its form is finally a matter for the designer, but to some extent is dictated by the action of the play. I have visualized two galleries of flattened Tudor arches, one above the other, able to be entered from off-stage. A flight of stairs leading from the upper gallery to the stage. A projection which can suggest an alcove or closet, with a tapestry curtain to be drawn across it. A table and some chairs, sufficiently heavy to be congruous indoors or out.

THE COSTUMES are also a matter for the designer, but I have visualized no exact reproductions of the elaborate style of the period. I think plain colors should be used, thus scarlet for the Cardinal, gray for More, gold for the King, green for the Duke, blue for Margaret, black and pinstripe for the administrators Rich and Cromwell, and so on.

ACT ONE

When the curtain rises, the set is in darkness but for a single spot upon the COMMON MAN, *who sits on a big property basket.*

COMMON MAN (*Rises*) It is perverse! To start a play made up of Kings and Cardinals in speaking costumes and intellectuals with embroidered mouths, with me.

If a King or a Cardinal had done the prologue he'd have had the right materials. And an intellectual would have shown enough majestic meanings, colored propositions, and closely woven liturgical stuff to dress the House of Lords! But this!

Is this a costume? Does this say anything? It barely covers one man's nakedness! A bit of black material to reduce Old Adam to the Common Man.

Oh, if they'd let me come on naked, I could have shown you something of my own. Which would have told you without words—! Something I've forgotten . . . Old Adam's muffled up. (*Backing towards the basket*) Well, for a proposition of my own, I need a costume. (*Takes out and puts on the coat and hat of* STEWARD) Matthew! The Household Steward of Sir Thomas More! (*Lights come up swiftly on set. He takes from the basket five silver goblets, one larger than the others, and a jug with a lid, with which he furnishes the table. A burst of conversational merriment off; he pauses and indicates head of stairs*) There's company to dinner. (*He pours a cup of wine*) All right! A Common Man! A Sixteenth-Century Butler! (*He drinks from the cup*) All right—the Six—— (*He breaks off, agreeably surprised by the quality of the liquor, regards the jug respectfully and drinks again from jug*) The Sixteenth Century is the Cen-

3

tury of the Common Man. (*He puts down the jug*) Like all
the other centuries. And that's my proposition.
(*During the last part of the speech, voices are heard off.
Now, enter, at the head of the stairs,* SIR THOMAS MORE)

STEWARD   That's Sir Thomas More.

MORE   The wine please, Matthew?

STEWARD   It's there, Sir Thomas.

MORE (*Looking into the jug*)   Is it good?

STEWARD   Bless you, sir! I don't know.

MORE (*Mildly*)   Bless you too, Matthew.
(*Enter* RICH *at the head of the stairs*)

RICH (*Enthusiastically pursuing an argument*)   But every man
has his price!

MORE   No-no-no—

STEWARD (*Contemptuously*)   Master Richard Rich.

RICH   But yes! In money too.

MORE (*With gentle impatience*)   No no no.

RICH   Or pleasure. Titles, women, bricks-and-mortar, there's
always something.

MORE   Childish.

4

RICH Well, in suffering, certainly.

MORE (*Interested*) Buy a man with suffering?

RICH Impose suffering, and offer him—escape.

MORE Oh. For a moment I thought you were being profound.
(*He gives a cup to* RICH)

RICH (*To* STEWARD) Good evening, Matthew.

STEWARD (*Snubbing*) 'Evening, sir.

RICH No, not a bit profound; it then becomes a purely practical question of how to make him suffer sufficiently.

MORE Mm . . . (*He takes him by the arm and walks with him*) And . . . who recommended you to read Signor Machiavelli? (RICH *breaks away laughing—a fraction too long.* MORE *smiles*) No, who? (*More laughter*) . . . Mm?

RICH Master Cromwell.

MORE Oh . . . (*He goes back to the wine jug and cups*) He's a very able man.

RICH And so he is!

MORE Yes, I say he is. He's very able.

RICH And he will do something for me, he says.

MORE   I didn't know you knew him.

RICH   Pardon me, Sir Thomas, but how much do you know about me?

MORE   Whatever you've let me know.

RICH   I've let you know everything!

MORE   Richard, you should go back to Cambridge; you're deteriorating.

RICH   Well, I'm not used! . . . D'you know how much I have to show for seven months' work—

MORE   Work?

RICH   Work! Waiting's work when you wait as I wait, hard! . . . For seven months, that's two hundred days, I have to show: the acquaintance of the Cardinal's outer doorman, the indifference of the Cardinal's inner doorman, and the Cardinal's chamberlain's hand in my chest! . . . Oh—also one half of a Good Morning delivered at fifty paces by the Duke of Norfolk. Doubtless he mistook me for someone.

MORE   He was very affable at dinner.

RICH   Oh, everyone's affable *here* . . . (MORE *is pleased*) Also, of course, the friendship of Sir Thomas More. Or should I say acquaintance?

MORE   Say friendship.

RICH Well, there! "A friend of Sir Thomas and still no office? There must be something wrong with him."

MORE I thought we said friendship . . . (*He considers; then*) The Dean of St. Paul's offers you a post; with a house, a servant and fifty pounds a year.

RICH What? What post?

MORE At the new school.

RICH (*Bitterly disappointed*) A teacher!

MORE A man should go where he won't be tempted. Look, Richard, see this. (*He hands him a silver cup*) Look . . . Look . . .

RICH Beautiful.

MORE Italian . . . Do you want it?

RICH Why?

MORE No joke; keep it; or sell it.

RICH Well— Thank you, of course. Thank you! Thank you! But—

MORE You'll sell it, won't you?

RICH Well—I— Yes, I will.

MORE And buy, what?

RICH (*With sudden ferocity*) Some decent clothes!

MORE (*With sympathy*) Ah.

RICH I want a gown like yours.

MORE You'll get several gowns for that I should think. It was sent to me a little while ago by some woman. Now she's put a lawsuit into the Court of Requests. It's a bribe, Richard.

RICH Oh . . . (*Chagrined*) So you give it away, of course.

MORE Yes!

RICH To me?

MORE Well, I'm not going to keep it, and you need it. Of course—if you feel it's contaminated . . .

RICH No, no. I'll risk it.
(*They both smile*)

MORE But, Richard, in office they offer you all sorts of things. I was once offered a whole village, with a mill, and a manor house, and heaven knows what else—a coat of arms, I shouldn't be surprised. Why not be a teacher? You'd be a fine teacher. Perhaps even a great one.

RICH And if I was, who would know it?

MORE You, your pupils, your friends, God. Not a bad public, that . . . Oh, and a *quiet* life.

RICH (*Laughing*) *You* say that!

MORE Richard, I was commanded into office; it was inflicted on me . . . (RICH *regards him*) Can't you believe that?

RICH It's hard.

MORE (*Grimly*) Be a teacher.

NORFOLK (*Enters at the head of the stairs*) It was magnificent!

STEWARD (*To audience*) The Duke of Norfolk. Earl Marshal of England.

NORFOLK I tell you he stooped from the clouds! (*Breaks off; irritably*) Alice!
(ALICE *enters instantly at the head of the stairs*)

ALICE (*Irritably*) Here!

STEWARD (*To audience*) Lady Alice. My master's wife.

NORFOLK I tell you he stooped—

ALICE He didn't—

NORFOLK Goddammit, he did—

ALICE Couldn't—

NORFOLK He *does*—

ALICE Not possible—

NORFOLK But *often*—

ALICE Never.

NORFOLK Well, damn my soul.

MORE (*To* MARGARET, *who has appeared on the gallery*) Come down, Meg.

STEWARD (*Soapy; to audience*) Lady Margaret, my master's daughter; lovely, really lovely.

ALICE (*Glances suspiciously at* STEWARD) Matthew, get about your business. (STEWARD *exits*) We'll settle this, my lord, we'll put it to Thomas. Thomas, no falcon could stoop from a cloud, could it?

MORE I don't know, my dear; it sounds unlikely. I have seen falcons do some very splendid things.

ALICE But how could he stoop from a cloud? He couldn't see where he was going.

NORFOLK You see, Alice—you're ignorant of the subject; a real falcon don't *care* where he's going! (*He takes some wine*) Thank you, Thomas. Anyway, I'm talking to Meg. (*A sportsman's story*) 'Twas the very first cast of the day, Meg; the sun was behind us. And from side to side of the valley like the roof of a tent was solid mist—

ALICE   Oh, mist.

NORFOLK   Well, mist is cloud, isn't it?

ALICE   No.

RICH   The opinion of Aristotle is that mists are an exhalation of the earth whereas clouds—

NORFOLK   He stooped five hundred feet! Like that! Like an Act of God, isn't he, Thomas?

MORE   He's tremendous.

NORFOLK (*To* ALICE)   Tremendous.

MARGARET   Did he kill the heron?

NORFOLK   Oh, the *heron* was *clever*. (*Very evidently discreditable*) It was a royal stoop though. (*Slyly*) If you could ride, Alice, I'd show you.

ALICE (*Hotly*)   I can ride, my lord!

MORE   No, no, you'll make yourself ill.

ALICE   And I'll bet—twenty-five—no, thirty shillings I see no falcon stoop from no cloud!

NORFOLK   Done.

MORE   Alice—you can't ride with *them*.

ALICE God's body, Thomas, remember who you are. Am I a city wife?

MORE No indeed, you've just lost thirty shillings, I think; there *are* such birds. And the heron got home to his chicks, Meg, so everything was satisfactory.

MARGARET (*Smiling*) Yes.

MORE What was that of Aristotle's, Richard?

RICHARD Nothing, Sir Thomas—'twas out of place.

NORFOLK (*To* RICH) I've never found much use in Aristotle myself, not practically. Great philosopher, of course. Wonderful mind.

RICH Exactly, Your Grace!

NORFOLK (*Suspicious*) Eh?

MORE Master Rich is newly converted to the doctrines of Machiavelli.

RICH Oh *no* . . . !

NORFOLK Oh, the Italian. Nasty book, from what I hear.

MARGARET Very practical, Your Grace.

NORFOLK You read it? Amazing girl, Thomas, but where are you going to find a husband for her?

Olga Bellin, Paul Scofield, Albert Dekker, William Redfield, and Carol Goodner, as MARGARET MORE, SIR THOMAS MORE, THE DUKE OF NORFOLK, RICHARD RICH, and ALICE MORE.

MORE (MORE *and* MEG *exchange a glance*) Where indeed?

RICH The doctrines of Machiavelli have been largely mistaken, I think; indeed, properly apprehended, he has no doctrine. Master Cromwell has the sense of it I think when he says—

NORFOLK You know Cromwell?

RICH . . . Slightly, Your Grace . . .

NORFOLK The Cardinal's Secretary.
(*Exclamations of shock from* MORE, MARGARET *and* ALICE)

ALICE Never—it can't be.

MARGARET The Cardinal's—it's impossible.

MORE Not possible!

NORFOLK It's a fact.

MORE When, Howard?

NORFOLK Two, three days.
(*They move about uneasily*)

ALICE A *farrier's* son?

NORFOLK Well, the Cardinal's a butcher's son, isn't he?

ALICE It'll be up quick and down quick with Master Cromwell.

(NORFOLK *grunts*)

MORE (*Quietly*) Did you know this?

RICH No!

MARGARET Do you *like* Master Cromwell, Master Rich?

ALICE He's the only man in London if he does!

RICH I think I do, Lady Alice!

MORE (*Pleased*) Good . . . Well, you don't need *my* help now.

RICH Sir Thomas, if only you knew how much, much rather I'd yours than his!
(*Enter* STEWARD, *who gives a letter to* MORE, *who opens it and reads*)

MORE Talk of the Cardinal's Secretary and the Cardinal appears. He wants me. Now.

ALICE At this time of the night?

MORE (*Mildly*) The King's business.

ALICE The Queen's business.

NORFOLK More than likely, Alice, more than likely.

MORE (*Cuts in sharply*) What's the time?

STEWARD Eleven o'clock, sir.

MORE Is there a boat?

STEWARD Waiting, sir.

MORE (*To* ALICE *and* MARGARET) Go to bed. You'll excuse me, Your Grace? Richard? Now you'll go to bed . . .
(*The* MORE *family, as a matter of routine, put their hands together*)

MORE, ALICE, MARGARET Dear Lord, give us rest tonight, or if we must be wakeful, cheerful. Careful only for our soul's salvation. For Christ's sake. Amen.

MORE And bless our Lord the King.

ALICE and MARGARET And bless our Lord the King.

ALL Amen.
(*And then immediately a brisk leave-taking:* MORE *moving off below, the others mounting the stairs*)

MORE Howard, are *you* at Richmond?

NORFOLK No, down the river.

MORE Then good night! (*He sees* RICH *disconsolate*) Oh, Your Grace, here's a young man desperate for employment. Something in the clerical line.

NORFOLK Well, if you recommend him.

MORE No. I don't recommend him; but I point him out. (*Moving off*) He's at the New Inn. Can you take him there?

NORFOLK (*To* RICH; *mounting the stairs*) All right, come on.

RICH My Lord.

NORFOLK We'll hawk at Hounslow, Alice.
ALICE Wherever you like.
  (ALICE *and* MARGARET *follow* NORFOLK)

RICH (*At foot of the stairs*) Sir Thomas! . . . (MORE *turns*) Thank you.

MORE Be a teacher. (*Moving off again*) Alice! The ground's hard at Hounslow!

NORFOLK Eh? (*Delighted roar*) That's where the Cardinal crushed his bum!

MORE, NORFOLK, ALICE, RICH Good night! Good night!
  (*They process off along the gallery*)

MORE (*Softly*) Margaret!

MARGARET Yes?

MORE Go to bed.
  (MARGARET *exits above*, MORE *exits below. After a moment* RICH *walks swiftly back, picks up the goblet and is going off with it*)

STEWARD (*Takes goblet*) Eh!

RICH What— Oh . . . It's a gift, Matthew. Sir Thomas gave it to me. (STEWARD *regards it silently*) He gave it to me.

STEWARD (*Returns it*) Very nice present, sir.

RICH (*Beginning to leave with it*) Yes. Good night, Matthew.

STEWARD Sir Thomas has taken quite a fancy to you, sir.

RICH Er, here—
(*Gives him some money and goes*)

STEWARD Thank you, sir . . . (*To audience*) That one'll come to nothing. (*Begins packing props into basket. Pauses with a cup in hand*) My master Thomas More would give anything to anyone. Some say that's good and some say that's bad, but I say he can't help it—and that's bad . . . because some day someone's going to ask him for something that he wants to keep; and he'll be out of practice. (*Puts a cloth, papers, pen and ink, and candles on the table*) There must be something that he wants to keep. That's only common sense.
(*Enter* WOLSEY. *He sits at the table and immediately commences writing, watched by* COMMON MAN, *who then exits. Enter* MORE)

WOLSEY (*Writing*) It's half-past one. Where've you been?
(*A bell strikes one*)

MORE   One o'clock, Your Grace. I've been on the river.
(WOLSEY *writes in silence while* MORE *waits standing*)

WOLSEY (*Still writing, pushes paper across the table*)   Since you seemed so violently opposed to the dispatch for Rome, I thought you'd like to look it over.

MORE (*Touched*)   Thank you, Your Grace.

WOLSEY   Before it goes.

MORE (*Smiles*)   Your Grace is very kind. (*He takes it and reads*) Thank you.

WOLSEY   Well, what d'you think of it?
(*He is still writing*)

MORE   It seems very well phrased, Your Grace.

WOLSEY (*Permits himself a chuckle*)   The devil it does! (*He sits back*) And apart from the style, Sir Thomas?

MORE (*Crisply*)   It's addressed to Cardinal Campeggio.

WOLSEY   Yes?

MORE   Not to our ambassador.

WOLSEY   Our ambassador's a ninny.

MORE (*A smile*)   Your Grace appointed him.

WOLSEY (*Treats it at the level of humor, mock exasperation*) Yes I need a *ninny* in Rome! So that I can write to Cardinal Campeggio!

MORE (*Won't respond; with aesthetic distaste—not moral disapproval*) It's devious.

WOLSEY It's a devious situation!

MORE There must be something simple in the middle of it. (*Again this is not a moral dictum; it is said rather wistfully, as of something he is beginning to doubt*)

WOLSEY (*After a pause, rather gently*) I believe you believe that. (*Briskly*) You're a constant regret to me, Thomas. If you could just see facts flat on, without that horrible moral squint; with just a little common sense, you could have been a statesman.

MORE (*After a little pause*) Oh, Your Grace flatters me.

WOLSEY Don't frivol . . . Thomas, are you going to help me?

MORE (*Hesitates, looks away*) If Your Grace will be specific.

WOLSEY Ach, you're a plodder! Take you altogether, Thomas, your scholarship, your experience, what are you? (*A single trumpet calls, distant, frosty and clear.* WOLSEY *gets up and goes and looks from the window*) Come here. (MORE *joins him*) The King.

MORE Yes.

WOLSEY Where has he been? D'you know?

MORE I, Your Grace?

WOLSEY Oh, spare me your discretion. He's been to play in the mud again.

MORE (*Coldly*) Indeed.

WOLSEY Indeed! Indeed! Are you going to oppose me? (*Trumpet sounds again.* WOLSEY *visibly relaxes*) He's gone in . . . (*He leaves the window*) All right, we'll plod. The King wants a son; what are you going to do about it?

MORE (*Dry murmur*) I'm very sure the King needs no advice from me on what to do about it.

WOLSEY (*From behind, grips his shoulder fiercely*) Thomas, we're alone. I give you my word. There's no one here.

MORE I didn't suppose there was, Your Grace.

WOLSEY Oh. Sit down! (*He goes to the table, sits, signals* MORE *to sit.* MORE *unsuspectingly obeys. Then, deliberately loud*) Do you favor a change of dynasty, Sir Thomas? D'you think two Tudors is sufficient?

MORE (*Starting up in horrified alarm*) For God's sake, Your Grace—

WOLSEY Then the King needs a son; I repeat, what are you going to do about it?

MORE (*Steadily*) I pray for it daily.

WOLSEY (*Softly*) God's death, he means it . . . That thing out there's at least fertile, Thomas.

MORE But she's not his wife.

WOLSEY No, Catherine's his wife and she's as barren as a brick. Are you going to pray for a miracle?

MORE There *are* precedents.

WOLSEY Yes. All right. Good. Pray. Pray by all means. But in addition to prayer there is effort. My effort's to secure a divorce. Have I your support or have I not?

MORE (*Sits*) A dispensation was granted so that the King might marry Queen Catherine, for state reasons. Now we are to ask the Pope to—dispense with his dispensation, also for state reasons?

WOLSEY I don't *like* plodding, Thomas, don't make me plod longer than I have to— Well?

MORE Then clearly all we have to do is approach His Holiness and ask him.
(*The pace becomes rapid*)

WOLSEY I think we might influence His Holiness' answer—

MORE Like this?
(*Indicating the dispatch*)

WOLSEY Like that and in other ways—

MORE I've already expressed my opinion on this—

WOLSEY Then, good night! Oh, your conscience is your own affair; but you're a statesman! Do you *remember* the Yorkist Wars?

MORE Very clearly.

WOLSEY Let him die without an heir and we'll have them back again. Let him die without an heir and this "peace" you think so much of will go out like that! (*He extinguishes the candle*) Very well then . . . England needs an heir; certain measures, perhaps regrettable, perhaps not— (*Pompous*) there is much in the Church that *needs* reformation, Thomas— (MORE *smiles*) All right, regrettable! But necessary, to get us an heir! Now explain how you as Councilor of England can obstruct those measures for the sake of your own, private, conscience.

MORE Well . . . I believe, when statesmen forsake their own private conscience for the sake of their public duties . . . they lead their country by a short route to chaos. (*During this speech he relights the candle with another*) And we shall have my prayers to fall back on.

WOLSEY You'd like that, wouldn't you? To govern the country by prayers?

MORE Yes, I should.

WOLSEY I'd like to be there when you try. Who *will*? (*He half lifts the chain from his shoulders*) Who will put his neck in this—after me? You? Tunstall? Suffolk?

MORE Tunstall for me.

WOLSEY Aye, but for the King. What about my Secretary, Master Cromwell?

MORE Cromwell!

WOLSEY You'd rather do it yourself?

MORE Me rather than Cromwell.

WOLSEY Then come down to earth, Thomas. (*He looks away*) And until you do, bear in mind you have an enemy!

MORE (*Wishing to make sure, quietly*) Where, Your Grace?

WOLSEY (*Looks back at him, hard-faced, harsh; for the first time we see this is a carnivore*) Here, Thomas.

MORE As Your Grace pleases.

WOLSEY As God wills!

MORE Perhaps, Your Grace.
(*Mounting stairs*)

WOLSEY More! You should have been a cleric!

MORE (*Amused, looking down from gallery*) Like yourself, Your Grace?

(*Exit* MORE. WOLSEY *is left staring, then exits through the lower arches with candle, taking most of the light from the stage as he does so. But the whole rear of the stage is now patterned with webbed reflections thrown from brightly moonlit water, so that the structure is thrown into black relief, while a strip of light descends along the front of the stage, which is to be the acting area for the next scene. An oar and a bundle of clothing are lowered into this area from above. Enter* COMMON MAN; *he unties the bundle and begins to don the coat and hat of* BOATMAN)

MORE (*Off*) Boat! Boat! (*Approaching*) Boat!

BOATMAN (*Donning coat and hat*) Here, sir!

MORE (*Off*) A boatman please!

BOATMAN Boat here, sir!
(*He seizes the oar. Enter* MORE)

MORE (*Peering*) Boatman?

BOATMAN Yes, sir. (*To audience, indicating oar*) A boatman.

MORE Take me home.

BOATMAN (*Pleasantly*) I was just going home myself, sir.

MORE Then find me another boat.

BOATMAN Bless you, sir—that's all right. (*Comfortably*) I expect you'll make it worth my while, sir.

CROMWELL (*Stepping from behind an arch*) Boatman, have you a license?

BOATMAN Eh? Bless you, sir, yes; I've got a license.

CROMWELL Then you know that the fares are fixed— (*Turns to* MORE. *Exaggerated pleasure*) Why, it's Sir Thomas!

MORE Good morning, Master Cromwell. You work very late.

CROMWELL I'm on my way to the Cardinal.

MORE (*Recollecting*) Ah yes, you are to be felicitated. Good morning, Master *Secretary*.
(*He smiles politely*)

CROMWELL (*Smiling*) Yes.

MORE If it *is* felicity to be busy in the night.

CROMWELL It is.

MORE Felicitations then.
(*They exchange a dry little bow*)

CROMWELL You have just left him, I think.

MORE Yes, I have.

CROMWELL You left him . . . in his laughing mood, I hope?

MORE   On the whole I would say not. No, not laughing.

CROMWELL   Oh, I'm sorry. (*Backing to exit*) I am one of your *multitudinous* admirers, Sir Thomas. A penny ha'penny to Chelsea, Boatman.
(*Exit* CROMWELL)

BOATMAN   The coming man they say, sir.

MORE   Do they? Well, where's your boat?

BOATMAN   Just along the wharf, sir.
(*They are going when* CHAPUYS *and his* ATTENDANT *enter*)

CHAPUYS   Sir Thomas More!

MORE   Signor Chapuys? You're up very late, Your Excellency.

CHAPUYS (*Significantly*)   So is the Cardinal, Sir Thomas.

MORE (*Closing up*)   He sleeps very little.

CHAPUYS   You have just left him, I think.

MORE   You are correctly informed. As always.

CHAPUYS   I will not ask you the subject of your conversation . . .
(*He waits*)

MORE   No, of course not.

CHAPUYS Sir Thomas, I will be plain with you . . . plain, that is, so far as the diplomatic decencies permit. (*Loudly*) My master Charles, the King of Spain! (*Pulls* MORE *aside; discreetly*) My master Charles, the King of Spain, feels himself concerned in anything concerning his blood relations. He would feel himself insulted by any insult offered to his mother's sister! I refer, of course, to Queen Catherine. (*He regards* MORE *keenly*) The King of Spain would feel himself insulted by any insult offered to Queen Catherine.

MORE His feeling would be natural.

CHAPUYS (*Consciously shy*) Sir Thomas, may I ask if you and the Cardinal parted, how shall I say, amicably?

MORE Amicably . . . Yes.

CHAPUYS (*A shade indignant*) In agreement?

MORE Amicably.

CHAPUYS (*Warmly*) Say no more, Sir Thomas; I understand.

MORE (*A bit worried*) I hope you do, Your Excellency.

CHAPUYS You are a good man.

MORE I don't see how you deduce that from what I told you.

CHAPUYS (*Holds up a hand*) A nod is as good as a wink to a blind horse. I understand. You are a good man. (*He turns to exit*) Dominus vobiscum.
(CHAPUYS *exits.* MORE *looks after him*)

27

MORE (*Abstracted*) . . . spiritu tuo . . .

BOATMAN (*Mournful; he is squatting on the ground*) Some
people think boats stay afloat on their own, sir, but they
don't; they cost money. (MORE *is abstractedly gazing over
the audience*) Take anchor rope, sir, you may not believe
me, for a little skiff like mine, but it's a penny a fathom.
(MORE *is still abstracted*) And with a young wife, sir, as
you know . . .

MORE (*Abstracted*) I'll pay what I always pay you . . . The
river looks very black tonight. They say it's silting up, is that
so?

BOATMAN (*Joining him*) Not in the middle, sir. There's a
channel there getting deeper all the time.

MORE How is your wife?

BOATMAN She's losing her shape, sir, losing it fast.

MORE Well, so are we all.

BOATMAN Oh yes, sir; it's common.

MORE (*Going*) Well, take me home.
  (*Exit* MORE)

BOATMAN That I will, sir! (*Crossing to the basket and pulling*
it out) From Richmond to Chelsea, a penny halfpenny . . .

(*He goes for the tablecloth*) from Chelsea to Richmond, a penny halfpenny. From Richmond to Chelsea, it's a quiet float downstream, from Chelsea to Richmond, it's a hard pull upstream. And it's a penny halfpenny either way. Whoever makes the regulations doesn't row a boat. (*Puts the cloth into the basket, takes out slippers*) Home again.
(*Lighting changes to* MORE's *house.* MORE *enters, sits wearily. He takes off hat, half takes off coat but is too tired. A bell chimes three.* STEWARD *kneels to put on his slippers for him*)

MORE   Ah, Matthew . . . Is Lady Alice in bed?

STEWARD   Yes, sir.

MORE   Lady Margaret?

STEWARD   No, sir. Master Roper's here.

MORE (*Surprised*)   At this hour? . . . Who let him in?

STEWARD   He's a hard man to keep out, sir.

MORE   Where are they?
    (MARGARET *and* ROPER *enter*)

MARGARET   Here, Father.

MORE   Thank you, Matthew. (STEWARD *exits.* MORE, *regarding them; resignedly*) Good morning, William. It's a little early for breakfast.

ROPER (*Stolidly*)   I haven't come for breakfast, sir.
(MORE *looks at him and sighs*)

MARGARET   Will wants to marry me, Father.

MORE   Well, he can't marry you.

ROPER   Sir Thomas, I'm to be called to the Bar.

MORE (*Warmly*)   Oh, congratulations, Roper!

ROPER   My family may not be at the palace, sir, but in the City—

MORE   The Ropers were advocates when the Mores were selling pewter; there's nothing wrong with your family. There's nothing wrong with your fortune—there's nothing wrong with you— (*Sourly*) except you need a clock—

ROPER   I can buy a clock, sir.

MORE   Roper, the answer's "no." (*Firmly*) And will be "no" so long as you're a heretic.

ROPER (*Firing*)   That's a word I don't like, Sir Thomas!

MORE   It's not a likable word. (*Coming to life*) It's not a likable thing!
(MARGARET *is alarmed, and from behind* MORE *tries to silence* ROPER)

ROPER   The Church is heretical! Doctor Luther's proved that to my satisfaction!

30

MORE Luther's an excommunicate.

ROPER From a heretic Church! Church? It's a shop— Forgiveness by the florin! Job lots now in Germany! . . . Mmmm, and divorces.

MORE (*Expressionless*) Divorces?

ROPER Oh, half England's buzzing with that.

MORE "Half England." The Inns of Court may be buzzing, England doesn't buzz so easily.

ROPER It will. And is that a Church? Is that a Cardinal? Is that a Pope? Or Antichrist! (MORE *looks up angrily.* MARGARET *signals frantically*) Look, what I know I'll say!

MARGARET You've no sense of the *place!*

MORE (*Rueful*) He's no sense of the time.

ROPER I—
(*But* MORE *gently holds up his hand and he stops*)

MORE Listen, Roper. Two years ago you were a passionate Churchman; now you're a passionate—Lutheran. We must just pray that when your head's finished turning, your face is to the front again.

ROPER Don't lengthen your prayers with *me*, sir!

MORE Oh, one more or less . . . Is your horse here?

ROPER   No, I walked.

MORE   Well, take a horse from the stables and get back home. (ROPER *hesitates*) Go along.

ROPER   May I come again?
(MORE *indicates* MARGARET)

MARGARET   Yes. Soon.

ROPER   Good night, sir.
(ROPER *exits*)

MARGARET   Is that final, Father?

MORE   As long as he's a heretic, Meg, that's absolute. (*Warmly*) Nice boy . . . Terribly strong principles though. I thought I told you to go to bed.

MARGARET   Yes, why?

MORE (*Lightly*)   Because I intended you to *go* to bed. You're very pensive?

MARGARET   You're very gay. Did the Cardinal talk about the divorce?

MORE   Mm? You know I think we've been on the wrong track with Will— It's no good arguing with a Roper—

MARGARET   Father, did he?

MORE *Old* Roper was just the same. Now let him think he's going *with* the current and he'll turn round and start swimming in the opposite direction. What we want is a really substantial attack on the Church.

MARGARET We're going to get it, aren't we?

MORE Margaret, I'll not have you talk treason . . . And I'll not have you repeat lawyer's gossip. I'm a lawyer myself and I know what it's worth.

ALICE (*Off. Indignant and excited*) Thomas!

MORE Now look what you've done.
(ALICE *enters at the head of the stairs in her nightgown*)

ALICE Young Roper! I've just seen young Roper! On *my* horse.

MORE He'll bring it back, dear. He's been to see Margaret.

ALICE Oh—why you don't beat that girl!

MORE No, no, she's full of education—and it's a delicate commodity.

ALICE Mm! And more's the pity!

MORE Yes, but it's there now and think what it cost.
(*He sneezes*)

ALICE (*Pouncing*) Ah! Margaret—hot water.
(*Exit* MARGARET)

33

MORE   I'm sorry you were awakened, chick.

ALICE   I wasn't sleeping very deeply. Thomas—what **did** Wolsey want?

MORE (*Innocently*)   Young Roper asked me for Margaret.

ALICE   What! Impudence!

MORE   Yes, wasn't it?

ALICE   Old fox! What did he want, Thomas?

MORE   He wanted me to read a dispatch.

ALICE   Was that all?

MORE   A Latin dispatch.

ALICE   Oh! You don't want to talk about it?

MORE (*Gently*)   No.
(*Enter* MARGARET *with a cup, which she takes to* MORE)

ALICE   Norfolk was speaking for you as Chancellor before **he** left.

MORE   He's a dangerous friend then. Wolsey's Chancellor, God help him. We don't want another. (MARGARET *takes the cup to him; he sniffs it*) I don't want this.

ALICE   Drink it. Great men get colds in the head just the same as commoners.

MORE That's dangerous, leveling talk, Alice. Beware of the Tower.

ALICE Drink it!

MORE (*Rises*) I will, I'll drink it in bed.
(*They move to the stairs and ascend, talking*)

MARGARET Would you want to be Chancellor?

MORE No.

MARGARET That's what I said. But Norfolk said if Wolsey fell—

MORE (*No longer flippant*) If Wolsey fell, the splash would swamp a few small boats like ours. There will be no new Chancellors while Wolsey lives.
(*They exit above. The light is dimmed there and a bright spot descends below. Into this bright circle is thrown a great red robe and the Cardinal's hat. The* COMMON MAN *enters and roughly piles them into his basket. He then takes from his pocket a pair of spectacles and from the basket a book*)

COMMON MAN (*Reading*) "Whether we follow tradition in ascribing Wolsey's death to a broken heart, or accept Professor Larcomb's less feeling diagnosis of pulmonary pneumonia, its effective cause was the King's displeasure. He died at Leicester on 29 November, 1530, while on his way to the Tower under charge of High Treason.

"England's next Lord Chancellor was Sir Thomas More, a scholar and, by popular repute, a saint. His scholarship

35

is supported by his writings; saintliness is a quality less easy to establish. But from his willful indifference to realities which were obvious to quite ordinary contemporaries, it seems all too probable that he had it."

(*Exit* COMMON MAN. *As he goes, lights come up and a screen is lowered depicting Hampton Court.* CROMWELL *is sitting halfway up the stairs.* RICH *enters*)

CROMWELL Rich! (RICH *stops, sees him, and smiles willingly*) What brings you to Hampton?

RICH I came with the Duke last night, Master Cromwell. They're hunting again.

CROMWELL It's a kingly pastime, Master Rich. (*Both smile*) I'm glad you found employment. You're the Duke's Secretary, are you not?

RICH (*Flustered*) My work is mostly secretarial.

CROMWELL (*As if making an effort of memory*) Or is it his librarian you are?

RICH I do look after His Grace's library, yes.

CROMWELL Oh. Well, that's something. And I don't suppose you're bothered much by His Grace—in the library? (RICH *smiles uncertainly*) It's odd how differently men's fortunes flow. My late master, Wolsey, died in disgrace, and here I am in the King's own service. There you are in a *comparative* backwater—yet the new Lord Chancellor's an old friend of yours.

(*He looks at* RICH *directly*)

RICH (*Uncertain*) He isn't really my *friend*. . . .

CROMWELL Oh, I thought he was.
(*He gets up, prepares to go*)

RICH In a sense he is.

CROMWELL (*Reproachful*) Well, I always understood he set
you up in life.

RICH He recommended me to the Duke.

CROMWELL Ah yes. Are you very attached to His Grace's
library, or would you be free to accept an office?

RICH (*Suspicious*) Have you offices in gift?

CROMWELL (*Deprecating*) I am listened to by those who
have.

RICH Master Cromwell—what *is* it that you do for the King?
(*Enter* CHAPUYS)

CHAPUYS (*Roguish*) Yes, I should like to know that, Master
Cromwell.

CROMWELL Ah, Signor Chapuys. You've met His Excellency
Rich? (*He indicates* CHAPUYS) The Spanish Ambassador.
(*He indicates* RICH) The Duke of Norfolk's librarian.

CHAPUYS But how should we introduce *you*, Master Cromwell, if we had the happiness?

CROMWELL   Oh, sly! Do you notice how sly he is, Rich? Well, I suppose you would call me (*He suddenly turns*) "The King's Ear" . . . (*A deprecating shrug*) It's a useful organ, the ear. But in fact it's even simpler than that. When the King wants something done, I do it.

CHAPUYS   Ah. (*Mock interest*) But then why these Justices, Chancellors, Admirals?

CROMWELL   Oh, *they* are the constitution. Our ancient, English constitution. I merely do things.

CHAPUYS   For example, Master Cromwell. . . .

CROMWELL (*Admiring*)   O-ho—beware these professional diplomats. Well now, for example; next week at Deptford we are launching the *Great Harry*—one thousand tons, four masts, sixty-six guns, an overall length of one hundred and seventy-five feet; it's expected to be very effective—all this you probably know. However, you may not know that the King himself will guide her down the river; yes, the King himself will be her pilot. He will have assistance, of course, but he himself will be her pilot. He will have a pilot's whistle upon which he will blow, and he will wear in every respect a common pilot's uniform. Except for the material, which will be cloth of gold. These innocent fancies require more preparation than you might suppose and someone has to do it. (*He spreads his hands*) Meanwhile, I do prepare myself for higher things. I stock my mind.

CHAPUYS   Alas, Master Cromwell, don't we all? This ship for instance—it has fifty-six guns by the way, not sixty-six and only forty of them heavy. After the launching, I understand, the King will take his barge to Chelsea.

(CROMWELL'S *face darkens during this speech*)

CROMWELL (*Sharply*) Yes—

CHAPUYS To—

CROMWELL Sir Thomas More's.

CHAPUYS (*Sweetly*) Will you be there?

CROMWELL Oh no—they'll talk about the divorce. (*It is* CHAPUYS' *turn to be shocked.* RICH *draws away uneasily*) The King will ask him for an answer.

CHAPUYS (*Ruffled*) He has given his answer!

CROMWELL The King will ask him for another.

CHAPUYS Sir Thomas is a good son of the Church!

CROMWELL Sir Thomas is a man.
(*Enter* STEWARD. *Both* CROMWELL *and* CHAPUYS *look towards him sharply, then back at one another*)

CHAPUYS (*Innocently*) Isn't that his Steward now?

CROMWELL I believe it is. Well, good day, Your Excellency.

CHAPUYS (*Eagerly*) Good day, Master Cromwell.
(*He expects him to go*)

CROMWELL (*Standing firm*) Good day.

(*And* CHAPUYS *has to go.* CROMWELL *walks aside with furtive and urgent beckonings to* STEWARD *to follow.* RICH *follows but hangs off. Meanwhile* CHAPUYS *and his* ATTENDANT *have gone behind screen, beneath which their legs protrude clearly*)

STEWARD (*Conspiratorially*) Sir, Sir Thomas doesn't talk about it. (*He waits but* CROMWELL *remains stony*) He doesn't talk about it to his wife, sir.
(*He waits again*)

CROMWELL This is worth nothing.

STEWARD (*Significantly*) But he doesn't talk about it to Lady Margaret—that's his daughter, sir.

CROMWELL So?

STEWARD So he's worried, sir . . . (CROMWELL *is interested*) Frightened . . . (CROMWELL *takes out a coin but pauses suspiciously*) Sir, he goes *white* when it's mentioned!

CROMWELL (*Hands him the coin*) All right.

STEWARD (*Looks at the coin; reproachfully*) Oh, *sir!*

CROMWELL (*Waves him away*) Are you coming in my direction, Rich?

RICH (*Still hanging off*) No no.

CROMWELL I think you should, you know.

RICH *I* can't tell you anything!
(*Exit* CROMWELL *and* RICH *in separate directions.* CHAPUYS *and* ATTENDANT *come from behind screen*)

CHAPUYS (*Beckons* STEWARD) Well?

STEWARD Sir Thomas rises at six, sir, and prays for an hour and a half.

CHAPUYS Yes?

STEWARD During Lent, sir, he lived entirely on bread and water.

CHAPUYS Yes?

STEWARD He goes to confession twice a week, sir. Parish priest. Dominican.

CHAPUYS Ah. He is a true son of the Church.

STEWARD (*Soapy*) That he is, sir.

CHAPUYS What did Master Cromwell want?

STEWARD Same as you, sir.

CHAPUYS No man can serve two masters, Steward.

STEWARD   No indeed, sir; I serve *one*.
(*He pulls to the front an enormous cross until then hanging at his back on a length of string—a caricature of the ebony cross worn by* CHAPUYS)

CHAPUYS   Good, simple man. Here. (*Gives him a coin. Going*) Peace be with you.

STEWARD   And with you, sir.

CHAPUYS   Our Lord watch you.

STEWARD   You too, sir. (*Exit* CHAPUYS *and* ATTENDANT) That's a very religious man.
(*Enter* RICH)

RICH   Matthew! What does Signor Chapuys want?

STEWARD   I've no idea, sir.

RICH (*Gives him a coin*)   What did you tell him?

STEWARD   I told him that Sir Thomas says his prayers and goes to confession.

RICH   Why that?

STEWARD   That's what he wanted to know, sir. I mean I could have told him any number of things about Sir Thomas— that he has rheumatism, prefers red wine to white, is easily seasick, fond of kippers, afraid of drowning. But that's what he wanted to know, sir.

RICH What did he say?

STEWARD He said that Sir Thomas is a good churchman, sir.

RICH (*Going*) Well, that's true, isn't it?

STEWARD I'm just telling you what he said, sir. Oh, uh, Master Cromwell went that way, sir.

RICH (*Furious*) Did I ask you which way Master Cromwell went?
(RICH *exits in opposite direction*)

STEWARD (*To audience, thoughtfully*) The great thing's not to get out of your depth . . . What I can tell them's common knowledge! But now they've given money for it and everyone wants value for his money. They'll make a secret of it now to prove they've not been bilked . . . They'll make it a secret by making it dangerous . . . Mm . . . Oh, when I can't touch the bottom I'll go deaf, blind and dumb. (*He holds out coins*) And that's more than I *earn* in a fortnight!
(*A fanfare of trumpets; the rear of the stage becomes a source of glittering blue light; Hampton Court is hoisted out of sight, and a rosebay is lowered. As the fanfare ceases,* NORFOLK, ALICE, MARGARET, *erupt onto the stage*)

ALICE (*With chain of office which she puts on table. Distressed*) No sign of him, my lord!

NORFOLK God's body, Alice, he must be found!

ALICE (*To* MEG) He *must* be in the house!

MARGARET He's *not* in the house, Mother!

ALICE Then he must be here in the garden!
(*They "search" among the screens*)

NORFOLK He takes things too far, Alice.

ALICE Do I not know it?

NORFOLK It will end badly for him!

ALICE I know that too!
(*They "notice" the* STEWARD)

NORFOLK Where's your master?

MARGARET Matthew! Where's my father? } (*Together*)

ALICE Where is Sir Thomas?
(*Fanfare, shorter but nearer*)

NORFOLK (*Despairing*) Oh, my God.

ALICE Oh, Jesus!

STEWARD My lady—the King?

NORFOLK Yes, fool! (*Threatening*) And if the King **arrives**
and the Chancellor's not here—

STEWARD Sir, my lady, it's not *my* fault!

NORFOLK (*Quietly displeased*)   Lady Alice, Thomas'll get **no** good of it. This is not how Wolsey made himself great.

ALICE (*Stiffly*)   Thomas has his own way of doing things, my lord!

NORFOLK (*Testily*)   Yes yes, Thomas is unique; but where *is* Thomas?
(STEWARD *swings onstage a small Gothic door. Plainsong is heard. All run to the door.* NORFOLK *opens it*)

ALICE   Thomas!

STEWARD   Sir!

MARGARET   Father!

NORFOLK (*Indignantly*)   My Lord Chancellor! (MORE *enters through the doorway. He blinks in the light. He is wearing a cassock; he shuts the door behind him*) What sort of fooling is this? Does the King visit you every day?

MORE   No, but I go to vespers most days.

NORFOLK   He's here!

MORE   But isn't this visit *meant* to be a surprise?

NORFOLK (*Grimly*)   For you, yes, not for him.

MARGARET   Father . . .
(*She indicates his cassock*)

45

NORFOLK Yes—d'you propose to meet the King disguised as a parish clerk? (*They fall upon him to drag the cassock over his head*) A parish clerk, my Lord Chancellor! You dishonor the King and his office!

MORE (*Appearing momentarily from the folds of the cassock*) The service of God is not a dishonor to any office. (*The cassock is pulled off*) Believe me, my friend, I do not belittle the honor His Majesty is doing me. (*Briskly*) Well! That's a lovely dress, Alice; so's that, Margaret. (*He looks at* NORFOLK) I'm a dowdy bird, aren't I? (*Looks at* ALICE) Calm yourself. (STEWARD *swings the door offstage*) Alice, we're all ready now.
(*He turns about and we see that his gown is caught up behind him revealing his spindly legs in long hose laced up at the thighs*)

ALICE Thomas!
(MARGARET *laughs*)

MORE What's the matter?
(*He turns around again and his womenfolk pursue him to pull down the gown while* NORFOLK *throws his hands in the air. Expostulation, explanation, exclamation overlap in a babble*)

NORFOLK By God, you can be harebrained!

MARGARET Be still!

ALICE Oh, Thomas! Thomas!
(MARGARET *spies chain of office, brings it to* MORE)

46

Carol Goodner, Paul Scofield, and Keith Baxter, as ALICE MORE,
SIR THOMAS MORE, and KING HENRY VIII

NORFOLK What whim possessed you—

MORE 'Twas not a whim!

ALICE Your second-best stockings!

MARGARET (*Offering the chain*) Father—

MORE (*Refusing*) No, no, no, no—

NORFOLK Oh, enough's enough!

MORE Haven't you done—
(*Fanfare—at the end of which* HENRY, *in a cloth of gold, runs out of the sunlight halfway down the steps and blows a blast on his pilot's whistle. All kneel. In the silence he descends slowly to their level, blowing softly*)

MORE Your Majesty does my house more honor than I fear my household can bear.

HENRY No ceremony, Thomas! No ceremony! (*They rise*) A passing fancy—I happened to be on the river. (*Holds out a shoe, proudly*) Look, mud.

MORE We do it in better style, Your Grace, when we come by the road.

HENRY Oh, the road! There's the road for me, Thomas, the river; *my* river . . . By heaven, what an evening! Lady Alice, I fear we come upon you unexpectedly.

ALICE (*Shocked*) Oh no, Your Grace— (*Remembering*) that is yes, but we are ready for you—ready to entertain Your Grace, that is.

MORE This is my daughter Margaret, sir. She has not had the honor to meet Your Grace.
(*She curtsys low*)

HENRY (*Looking her over*) Why, Margaret, they told me you were a scholar.
(MARGARET *is confused*)

MORE Answer, Margaret.

MARGARET Among women I pass for one, Your Grace.
(NORFOLK *and* ALICE *exchange approving glances*)

HENRY Antiquone modo Latine loqueris, an Oxoniensi?
[Is your Latin the old Latin, or Oxford Latin?]

MARGARET Quem me docuit pater, Domine.
[My father's Latin, Sire.]

HENRY Bene. Optimus est. Graecamne linguam quoque te docuit?
[Good. That is the best. And has he taught you Greek too?]

MARGARET Graecam me docuit non pater meus sed mei patris amicus, Johannes Coletus, Sancti Pauli Decanus. In litteris Graecis tamen, non minus quam Latinis, ars magistri minuitur discipuli stultitia.
[Not my father, Sire, but my father's friend, John Colet,

Dean of St. Paul's. But it is with the Greek as it is with the Latin; the skill of the master is lost in the pupil's lack of it.]

(*Her Latin is better than his; he is not altogether pleased*)

HENRY Ho! (*He walks away from her, talking; she begins to rise from her curtsy;* MORE *gently presses her down again before* KING HENRY *turns*) Take care, Thomas: "too much learning is a weariness of the flesh, and there is no end to the making of books." (*Back to* MARGARET) Can you dance, too?

MARGARET Not well, Your Grace.

HENRY Well, *I* dance superlatively! (*He plants his leg before her face*) That's a dancer's *leg*, Margaret! (*She has the wit to look straight up and smile at him. All good humor, he pulls her to her feet, sees* NORFOLK *grinning the grin of a comrade*) Hey, Norfolk? (*Indicates* NORFOLK's *leg with much distaste*) Now *that's* a wrestler's leg. But I can throw him. (*Seizes* NORFOLK) Shall I show them, Howard? (*NORFOLK is alarmed for his dignity. To* MARGARET) Shall I?

MARGARET (*Looking at* NORFOLK; *gently*) No, Your Grace.

HENRY (*Releases* NORFOLK; *seriously*) You are gentle. (*To* MORE, *approvingly*) That's good. (*To* MARGARET) You shall read to me. (*MARGARET is about to demur*) No no, you shall read to me. Lady Alice, the river's given me an appetite.

ALICE If Your Grace would share a very simple supper.

HENRY It would please me to. (*Preparing to lead off, sees* MARGARET *again*) I'm something of a scholar too, Margaret, did you know?

MARGARET All the world knows Your Grace's book, asserting the seven sacraments of the Church.

HENRY Ah yes. Between ourselves, your father had a hand in that; eh, Thomas?

MORE Here and there, Your Grace. In a minor capacity.

HENRY (*Looking at him*) He seeks to shame me with his modesty . . . (*Turns to* ALICE) On second thought we'll follow, Lady Alice, Thomas and I will follow. (*He waves them off. They bow, withdraw to the steps and start up*) Wait! (*Raises whistle to lips*) Margaret, are you fond of music?

MARGARET Yes, Your Grace.

HENRY (*Beckons her to him; holds out whistle*) Blow. (*She is uncertain*) Blow. (*She does*) Louder! (*She does and at once music is heard without, stately and oversweet. Expressions of pleasure all round*) I brought them with me, Lady Alice; take them in! (*Exit all but* MORE *and* HENRY. *The music begins to recede*) Listen to this, Thomas. (*He walks about, the auditor, beating time*) Do you know it?

MORE No, Your Grace, I—

HENRY Sh! (MORE *is silent;* HENRY *goes on with his listening*) . . . I launched a ship today, Thomas.

MORE   Yes, Your Grace, I—

HENRY   *Listen,* man, *listen* . . . (*A pause*) . . . The *Great Harry* . . . I steered her, Thomas, under sail.

MORE   You have many accomplishments, Your Grace.

HENRY (*Holds up a finger for silence. A pause*) A great experience. (MORE *keeps silent*) . . . A great experience, Thomas.

MORE   Yes, Your Grace.
(*The music is growing fainter*)

HENRY   I am a fool.

MORE   How so, Your Grace?

HENRY (*A pause, during which the music fades to silence*) What else but a fool to live in a Court, in a licentious mob— when I have friends, with gardens.

MORE   Your Grace—

HENRY   No courtship, no ceremony, Thomas. Be seated. You *are* my friend, are you not?
(MORE *sits*)

MORE   Your Majesty.

HENRY (*Eyes lighting on the chain on the table by* MORE) And thank God I have a friend for my Chancellor. (*Laugh-*

ingly, but implacably, he takes up the chain and lowers it over MORE's *head*) Readier to be friends, I trust, than he was to be Chancellor.

MORE   My own knowledge of my poor abilities—

HENRY   I will judge of your abilities, Thomas . . . Did you know that Wolsey named you for Chancellor?

MORE   Wolsey!

HENRY   Aye, before he died. Wolsey named you and Wolsey was no fool.

MORE   He was a statesman of incomparable ability, Your Grace.

HENRY   Was he? Was he so? (*He rises*) Then why did he fail me? Be seated—it was villainy then! Yes, villainy. I was right to break him; he was all pride, Thomas; a proud man; pride right through. And he failed me! (MORE *opens his mouth*) He failed me in the one thing that mattered! The one thing that matters, Thomas, then or now. And why? He wanted to be Pope! Yes, he wanted to be the Bishop of Rome. I'll tell you something, Thomas, and you can check this for yourself—it was never merry in England while we had Cardinals amongst us. (*He nods significantly at* MORE, *who lowers his eyes*) But look now— (*Walking away*) —I shall forget the feel of that . . . great tiller under my hands . . . I took her down to Dogget's Bank, went about and brought her up in Tilbury Roads. A man could sail clean round the world in that ship.

MORE (*With affectionate admiration*) Some men could, Your Grace.

HENRY (*Offhand*) Touching this matter of my divorce, Thomas; have you thought of it since we last talked?

MORE Of little else.

HENRY Then you see your way clear to me?

MORE That you should put away Queen Catherine, Sire? Oh, alas (*He thumps the chair in distress*) as I think of it I see so clearly that I can *not* come with Your Grace that my endeavor is not to think of it at all.

HENRY Then you have not thought enough! . . . (*With real appeal*) Great God, Thomas, why do you hold out against me in the desire of my heart—the very wick of my heart?

MORE (*Draws up his sleeve, baring his arm*) There is my right arm. (*A practical proposition*) Take your dagger and saw it from my shoulder, and I will laugh and be thankful, if by that means I can come with Your Grace with a clear conscience.

HENRY (*Uncomfortably pulls at the sleeve*) I know it, Thomas, I know . . .

MORE (*Rises, formally*) I crave pardon if I offend.

HENRY (*Suspiciously*) Speak then.

MORE   When I took the Great Seal your Majesty promised not
to pursue me on this matter.

HENRY   Ha! So I break my word, Master More! No no, I'm
joking . . . I joke roughly . . . (*He wanders away*) I often
think I'm a rough fellow . . . Yes, a rough young fellow.
(*He shakes his head indulgently*) Be seated . . . That's a
rosebay. We have one like it at Hampton—not so red as that
though. Ha—I'm in an excellent frame of mind. (*Glances at
the rosebay*) Beautiful. (*Reasonable, pleasant*) You must
consider, Thomas, that I stand in peril of my soul. It was no
marriage; she was my brother's widow. Leviticus: "Thou
shalt not uncover the nakedness of thy brother's wife." Leviticus, Chapter eighteen, Verse sixteen.

MORE   Yes, Your Grace. But Deuteronomy—

HENRY (*Triumphant*)   Deuteronomy's ambiguous!

MORE (*Bursting out*)   Your Grace, I'm not fit to meddle in
these matters—to me it seems a matter for the Holy See—

HENRY (*Reprovingly*)   Thomas, Thomas, does a man need a
Pope to tell him when he's sinned? It was a sin, Thomas;
I admit it; I repent. And God has punished me; I have no
son . . . Son after son she's borne me, Thomas, all dead at
birth, or dead within the month; I never saw the hand of
God so clear in anything . . . I have a daughter, she's a
good child, a well-set child— But I have no son. (*He flares
up*) It is my bounden *duty* to put away the Queen, and all
the Popes back to St. Peter shall not come between me and
my duty! How is it that you cannot see? Everyone else does.

MORE (*Eagerly*) Then why does Your Grace need my poor support?

HENRY Because you are honest. What's more to the purpose, you're known to be honest . . . There are those like Norfolk who follow me because I wear the crown, and there are those like Master Cromwell who follow me because they are jackals with sharp teeth and I am their lion, and there is a mass that follows me because it follows anything that moves—and there is you.

MORE I am sick to think how much I must displease Your Grace.

HENRY No, Thomas, I respect your sincerity. Respect? Oh, man, it's water in the desert . . . How did you like our music? That air they played, it had a certain—well, tell me what you thought of it.

MORE (*Relieved at this turn; smiling*) Could it have been Your Grace's own?

HENRY (*Smiles back*) Discovered! Now I'll never know your true opinion. And that's irksome, Thomas, for we artists, though we love praise, yet we love truth better.

MORE (*Mildly*) Then I will tell Your Grace truly what I thought of it.

HENRY (*A little disconcerted*) Speak then.

MORE To me it seemed—delightful.

HENRY Thomas—I chose the right man for Chancellor.

MORE I must in fairness add that my taste in music is reputedly deplorable.

HENRY Your taste in music is excellent. It exactly coincides with my own. Ah music! Music! Send them back without me, Thomas; I will live here in Chelsea and make music.

MORE My house is at Your Grace's disposal.

HENRY Thomas, you understand me; we will stay here together and make music.

MORE Will Your Grace honor my roof after dinner?

HENRY (*Walking away, blowing moodily on his whistle*) Mm? Yes, I expect I'll bellow for you . . .

MORE My wife will be more—

HENRY Yes, yes. (*He turns, his face set*) Touching this other business, mark you, Thomas, I'll have no opposition.

MORE (*Sadly*) Your Grace?

HENRY No opposition, I say! No opposition! Your conscience is your own affair; but you are my Chancellor! There, you have my word—I'll leave you out of it. But I don't take it kindly, Thomas, and I'll have no opposition! I see how it will be; the bishops will oppose me. The full-fed, hypocritical, "Princes of the *Church*"! Ha! As for the Pope! Am I to burn in Hell because the Bishop of Rome, with the King of Spain's knife to his throat, mouths me Deuteronomy? Hypocrites! They're all hypocrites! Mind they do not take you in, Thomas! Lie low if you will, but I'll brook no opposition—no noise! No words, no signs, no letters, no pamphlets— Mind that, Thomas—no writings against me!

MORE   Your Grace is unjust. I am Your Grace's loyal minister. If I cannot serve Your Grace in this great matter of the Queen—

HENRY   I have no Queen! Catherine is not my wife and no priest can make her so, and they that say she is my wife are not only liars . . . but traitors! Mind it, Thomas!

MORE   Am I a babbler, Your Grace?
(*But his voice is unsteady*)

HENRY   You are stubborn . . . (*Wooingly*) If you could come with me, you are the man I would soonest raise—yes, with my own hand.

MORE (*Covers his face*)   Oh, Your Grace overwhelms me!
(*A complicated chiming of little bells is heard*)

HENRY   What's that?

MORE   Eight o'clock, Your Grace.

HENRY (*Uneasily eying* MORE)   Oh, lift yourself up, man— have I not promised? (MORE *braces*) Shall we eat?

MORE If Your Grace pleases. (*Recovering*) What will Your Grace sing for us?

HENRY Eight o'clock you said? Thomas, the tide will be changing. I was forgetting the tide. I'd better go.

MORE (*Gravely*) I'm sorry, Your Grace.

HENRY I must catch the tide or I'll not get back to Richmond till . . . No, don't come. Tell Norfolk. (*He has his foot on the stairs when* ALICE *enters above*) Oh, Lady Alice, I must go. (ALICE *descends, her face serious*) I want to catch the tide. To tell the truth, Lady Alice, I have forgotten in your haven here how time flows past outside. Affairs call me to court and so I give you my thanks and say good night. (*He mounts*)

MORE and ALICE (*Bowing*) Good night, Your Grace.
(*Exit* HENRY, *above*)

ALICE What's this? You crossed him.

MORE Somewhat.

ALICE Why?

MORE (*Apologetic*) I couldn't find the other way.

ALICE (*Angrily*) You're too nice altogether, Thomas!

MORE Woman, mind your house.

58

ALICE I *am* minding my house!

MORE (*Taking in her anxiety*) Well, Alice. What would you *want* me to do?

ALICE Be ruled! If you won't rule him, be ruled!

MORE (*Quietly*) I neither could nor would rule my King. (*Pleasantly*) But there's a little . . . little, area . . . where I must rule myself. It's very little—less to him than a tennis court. (*Her face is still full of foreboding; he sighs*) Look; it was eight o'clock. At eight o'clock, Lady Anne likes to dance.

ALICE (*Relieved*) Oh?

MORE I think so.

ALICE (*With irritation*) And *you* stand between them!

MORE I? What stands between them is a sacrament of the Church. I'm less important than you think, Alice.

ALICE (*Appealing*) Thomas, stay friends with him.

MORE Whatever can be done by smiling, you may rely on me to do.

ALICE You don't know *how* to flatter.

MORE I flatter very well! My recipe's beginning to be widely copied. It's the basic syrup with just a soupçon of discreet impudence . . .

ALICE (*Still uneasy*) I wish he'd eaten here . . .

MORE Yes—we shall be living on that "simple supper" of yours for a fortnight. (*She won't laugh*) Alice . . . (*She won't turn*) Alice . . . (*She turns*) Set your mind at rest—this (*Tapping himself*) is not the stuff of which martyrs are made.
(*Enter above, quickly, ROPER*)

ROPER Sir Thomas!

MORE (*Winces*) Oh, no . . .
(*Enter after ROPER, MARGARET*)

ALICE Will Roper—what do you want?

MARGARET William, I told you not to!

ROPER I'm not easily "told," Meg.

MARGARET I *asked* you not to.

ROPER Meg, I'm full to here!
(*Indicates his throat*)

MARGARET It's not convenient!

ROPER Must everything be made convenient? I'm not a convenient man, Meg—I've got an inconvenient conscience!
(*MARGARET gestures helplessly to MORE*)

MORE (*Laughs*) Joshua's trumpet. One note on that brass conscience of yours and my daughter's walls are down.

ROPER (*Descending*) You raised her, sir.

MORE (*A bit puzzled*) How long have you been here? Are you in the King's party?

ROPER No, sir, I am *not* in the King's party! (*Advancing*) It's of that I wish to speak to you. My spirit is perturbed.

MORE (*Suppressing a grin*) It is, Will? Why?

ROPER I've been offered a seat in the next Parliament. (MORE *looks up sharply*) Ought I to take it?

MORE No . . . Well that depends. With your views on Church Reform I should have thought you could do yourself a lot of good in the next Parliament.

ROPER My views on the Church, I must confess— Since last we met my views have somewhat modified. (MORE *and* MARGARET *exchange a smile*) I modify nothing concerning the *body* of the Church—the money-changers in the temple must be scourged from thence—with a scourge of fire if that is needed! But an attack on the Church herself! No, I see behind that an attack on God—

MORE Roper—

ROPER The Devil's work!

MORE Roper!

ROPER To be done by the Devil's ministers!

MORE   For heaven's sake remember my office!

ROPER   Oh, if you stand on your office—

MORE   I don't stand on it, but there are certain things I may not hear!

ROPER   Sophistication. It is what I was told. The Court has corrupted you, Sir Thomas; you are not the man you were; you have learned to study your "convenience"; you have learned to flatter!

MORE   There, Alice, you see? I have a reputation for it.

ALICE   God's Body, young man, if I was the Chancellor I'd have you whipped!
(*Enter* STEWARD)

STEWARD   Master Rich is here, Sir Thomas.
(RICH *follows him closely*)

RICH   Good evening, sir.

MORE   Ah, Richard?

RICH   Good evening, Lady Alice. (ALICE *nods, noncommittally*) Lady Margaret.

MARGARET (*Quite friendly but very clear*)   Good evening, Master Rich.
(*A pause*)

MORE   Do you know— (*Indicates* ROPER) William Roper, **the** younger?

RICH   By reputation, of course.

ROPER   Good evening, Master . . .

RICH   Rich.

ROPER   Oh. (*Recollecting something*) Oh.

RICH (*Quickly and hostilely*)   You have heard of me?

ROPER (*Shortly*)   Yes.

RICH (*Excitedly*)   In what connection? I don't know what you can have heard— (*He looks about; hotly*) I sense that I'm not welcome here!
(*He has jumped the gun; they are startled*)

MORE (*Gently*)   Why, Richard, have you done something that should make you not welcome?

RICH   Why, do you suspect me of it?

MORE   I shall begin to.

RICH (*Drawing closer to him and speaking hurriedly*)   Cromwell is asking questions. About you. About you particularly. (MORE *is unmoved*) He is continually collecting information about you!

MORE   I know it. (STEWARD *begins to slide out*) Stay a minute, Matthew.

RICH (*Pointing*)   That's one of his sources!

MORE   Of course; that's one of my servants.

RICH (*Hurriedly, in a low voice again*)   Signor Chapuys, the Spanish Ambassador—

MORE   —collects information too. That's one of his functions. (*He looks at* RICH *very gravely*)

RICH (*Voice cracking*)   You look at me as though I were an enemy!

MORE (*Putting out a hand to steady him*)   Why, Richard, you're shaking.

RICH   I'm adrift. Help me.

MORE   How?

RICH   Employ me.

MORE   No.

RICH (*Desperately*)   Employ me!

MORE   No!

RICH (*Moves swiftly to exit; turns*)   I would be steadfast!

64

MORE Richard, you couldn't answer for yourself even so far as tonight.

(RICH *exits. All watch him; the others turn to* MORE, *their faces alert*)

ROPER Arrest him.

ALICE Yes!

MORE For what?

ALICE He's dangerous!

ROPER For libel; he's a spy.

ALICE He is! Arrest him!

MARGARET Father, that man's bad.

MORE There is no law against that.

ROPER There is! God's law!

MORE Then God can arrest him.

ROPER Sophistication upon sophistication!

MORE No, sheer simplicity. The law, Roper, the law. I know what's legal not what's right. And I'll stick to what's legal.

ROPER Then you set man's law above God's!

MORE No, far below; but let me draw your attention to a

fact—I'm *not* God. The currents and eddies of right and wrong, which you find such plain sailing, I can't navigate. I'm no voyager. But in the thickets of the law, oh, there I'm a forester. I doubt if there's a man alive who could follow me there, thank God . . .
(*He says this last to himself*)

ALICE (*Exasperated, pointing after* RICH) While you talk, he's gone!

MORE   And go he should, if he was the Devil himself, until he broke the law!

ROPER   So now you'd give the Devil benefit of law!

MORE   Yes. What would you do? Cut a great road through the law to get after the Devil?

ROPER   I'd cut down every law in England to do that!

MORE (*Roused and excited*)   Oh? (*Advances on* ROPER) And when the last law was down, and the Devil turned round on you—where would you hide, Roper, the laws all being flat? (*He leaves him*) This country's planted thick with laws from coast to coast—man's laws, not God's—and if you cut them down—and you're just the man to do it—d'you really think you could stand upright in the winds that would blow then? (*Quietly*) Yes, I'd give the Devil benefit of law, for my own safety's sake.

ROPER   I have long suspected this; this is the golden calf; the law's your god.

MORE (*Wearily*)   Oh, Roper, you're a fool, God's my god. . . . (*Rather bitterly*) But I find him rather too (*Very bitterly*) subtle . . . I don't know where he is nor what he wants.

ROPER   My god wants service, to the end and unremitting; nothing else!

MORE (*Dryly*)   Are you sure that's God? He sounds like Moloch. But indeed it may be God— And whoever hunts for me, Roper, God or Devil, will find me hiding in the thickets of the law! And I'll hide my daughter with me! Not hoist her up the mainmast of your seagoing principles! They put about too nimbly!
(*Exit* MORE. *They all look after him.* MARGARET *touches* ROPER's *hand*)

MARGARET   Oh, that was harsh.

ROPER (*Turning to her; seriously*)   What's happened here?

ALICE (*Still with her back to them, her voice strained*)   He can't abide a fool, that's all! Be off!

ROPER (*To* MARGARET)   Hide you. Hide you from what?

ALICE (*Turning, near to tears*)   He said nothing about hiding me, you noticed! I've got too fat to hide, I suppose!

MARGARET   You know he meant us both.

ROPER   But from what?

ALICE   I don't know. I don't know if he knows. He's not said one simple, direct word to me since this divorce came **up**. It's not God who's gone subtle! It's him!

(*Enter* MORE, *a little sheepish. He goes to* ROPER)

MORE (*Kindly*) Roper, that was harsh: your principles are— (*He can't resist sending him up*) excellent—the very best quality. (ROPER *bridles. Contritely*) No, truly now, your principles are fine. (*Indicating the stairs, to all*) Look, we must make a start on all that food.

MARGARET Father, can't you be plain with us?

MORE (*Looks quickly from daughter to wife. Takes* ALICE'S *hand*) I stand on the wrong side of no statute, and no common law. (*Takes* MEG'S *hand too*) I have not disobeyed my sovereign. I truly believe no man in England is safer than myself. And I want my supper. (*He starts them up the stairs and goes to* ROPER) We shall need your assistance, Will. There's an excellent Burgundy—if your principles permit.

ROPER They don't, sir.

MORE Well, have some water in it.

ROPER Just the water, sir.

MORE My poor boy.

ALICE (*Stopping at the head of the stairs, as if she will be answered*) Why does Cromwell collect information about you?

MORE   I'm a prominent figure. Someone somewhere's collecting information about Cromwell. Now no more shirking; we
must make a start. (*Shepherding* ROPER *up the stairs*)
There's a stuffed swan if you please. (ALICE *and* MARGARET
exit above) Will, I'd trust *you* with my life. But not your
principles. (*They mount the stairs*) You see, we speak of
being anchored to our principles. But if the weather turns
nasty you up with an anchor and let it down where there's
less wind, and the fishing's better. And "Look," we say, "look,
I'm anchored!" (*Laughing, inviting* ROPER *to laugh with
him*) "To my principles!"
(*Exit above,* MORE *and* ROPER. *Enter* COMMON MAN *pulling
the basket. From it he takes an inn sign, which he hangs in
the alcove. He inspects it*)

COMMON MAN   "The Loyal Subject" . . . (*To audience*) A
pub. (*Takes from the basket and puts on a jacket, cap and
napkin*) A publican. (*Places two stools at the table, and on
it mugs and a candle, which he lights*) Oh, he's a deep one,
that Sir Thomas More . . . Deep . . . It takes a lot of education to get a man as deep as that . . . (*Straight to audience*) And a deep nature to begin with too. (*Deadpan*) The
likes of me can hardly be *expected* to follow the process of a
man like that. . . . (*Slyly*) Can we? (*He inspects the pub*)
Right, ready. (*He goes right*) Ready, sir!
(CROMWELL *enters, carrying a bottle*)

CROMWELL   Is this a *good* place for a conspiracy, innkeeper?

PUBLICAN (*Woodenly*)   You asked for a private room, sir.

CROMWELL (*Looking round*)   Yes, I want one without too
many little dark corners.

69

PUBLICAN   I don't understand you, sir. Just the four corners as you see.

CROMWELL (*Sardonically*)   You don't understand me.

PUBLICAN   That's right, sir.

CROMWELL   Do you know who I am?

PUBLICAN (*Promptly*)   No, sir.

CROMWELL   Don't be too tactful, innkeeper.

PUBLICAN   I don't understand, sir.

CROMWELL   When the likes of you *are* too tactful, the likes of me begin to wonder who's the fool.

PUBLICAN   I just don't understand you, sir.

CROMWELL (*Puts back his head and laughs silently*)   The master statesman of us all. "I don't understand." (*Looks at* PUBLICAN *almost with hatred*) All right. Get out. (*Exit PUBLICAN.* CROMWELL *goes to the exit. Calling*) Come on. (*Enter* RICH. *He glances at the bottle in* CROMWELL's *hand and remains cautiously by the exit*) Yes, it may be that I am a little intoxicated. (*Leaves* RICH *standing*) But not with alcohol, I've a strong head for that. With success! And who has a strong head for success? None of us gets enough of it. Except Kings. And they're born drunk.

RICH   Success? What success?

CROMWELL   Guess.

RICH   Collector of Revenues for York.

CROMWELL (*Amused*)   You do keep your ear to the ground, don't you? No.

RICH   What then?

CROMWELL   Sir Thomas Paget is—retiring.

RICH   Secretary to the Council!

CROMWELL   'Tis astonishing, isn't it?

RICH (*Hastily*)   Oh no—I mean—one sees, it's logical.

CROMWELL   No ceremony, no courtship. Be seated. (RICH *starts to sit*) As His Majesty would say. (RICH *jumps up— is pulled down, laughs nervously and involuntarily glances round*) Yes; see how I trust you.

RICH   Oh, I would never repeat or report a thing like that—

CROMWELL (*Pouring the wine*)   What kind of thing would you repeat or report?

RICH   Well, nothing said in friendship—may I say "friendship"?

CROMWELL   If you like. D'you believe that—that you would never repeat or report anything et cetera?

RICH Yes!

CROMWELL No, but seriously.

RICH Why, yes!

CROMWELL (*Puts down the bottle. Not sinister, but rather as a kindly teacher with a promising pupil*) Rich; seriously.

RICH (*Pauses, then bitterly*) It would depend what I was offered.

CROMWELL Don't say it just to please me.

RICH It's true. It would depend what I was offered.

CROMWELL (*Patting his arm*) Everyone knows it; not many people can say it.

RICH There are *some* things one wouldn't do for anything. Surely.

CROMWELL Mm—that idea's like these life lines they have on the embankment: comforting, but you don't expect to have to use them. (*Briskly*) Well, congratulations!

RICH (*Suspiciously*) On what?

CROMWELL I think you'd make a good Collector of Revenues for York Diocese.

RICH (*Gripping himself*) Is it in your gift?

CROMWELL It will be.

RICH (*With conscious cynicism*) What do I have to do for it?

CROMWELL Nothing. (*He lectures*) It isn't like that, Rich. There are no rules. With rewards and penalties—so much wickedness purchases so much worldly prospering— (*Rises. He breaks off and stops, suddenly struck*) Are you sure you're not religious?

RICH Almost sure.

CROMWELL Get sure. (*Resumes pacing up steps*) No, it's not like that, it's much more a matter of convenience, administrative convenience. The normal aim of administration is to keep steady this factor of convenience—and Sir Thomas would agree. Now normally when a man wants to change his woman, you let him if it's convenient and prevent him if it's not—normally indeed it's of so little importance that you leave it to the priests. But the constant factor is this element of convenience.

RICH Whose convenience?
(CROMWELL *stops*)

CROMWELL (*Sits*) Oh, ours. But everybody's too. However, in the present instance the man who wants to change his woman is our Sovereign Lord, Harry, by the Grace of God, the Eighth of that name. Which is a quaint way of saying that if he wants to change his woman he will. (*He rises and walks back towards* RICH) So *that* becomes the constant fac-

tor. And our job as administrators is to make it as convenient as we can. I say "our" job, on the assumption that you'll take this post at York I've offered you?
(*Makes* RICH *move over*)

RICH   Yes . . . yes, yes.
(*But he seems gloomy*)

CROMWELL (*Sits. Sharply*)   It's a bad sign when people are depressed by their own good fortune.

RICH (*Defensively*)   I'm not depressed!

CROMWELL   You look depressed.

RICH (*Hastily buffooning*)   I'm lamenting. I've lost my innocence.

CROMWELL   You lost that some time ago. If you've only just noticed, it can't have been very important to you.

RICH (*Much struck*)   That's true! Why that's true, it can't!

CROMWELL   We experience a sense of release, do we, Master Rich? An unfamiliar freshness in the head, as of open air?

RICH (*Takes the wine*)   Collector of Revenues isn't bad!

CROMWELL   Not bad for a start. (*He watches* RICH *drink*) Now our present Lord Chancellor—*there's* an innocent man.

RICH (*Indulgently*)   The odd thing is—he *is*.

74

CROMWELL (*Looks at him with dislike*) Yes, I say he is. (*With the light tone again*) The trouble is, his innocence is tangled in this proposition that you can't change your woman without a divorce, and can't have a divorce unless the Pope says so. And although his present Holiness is—judged even by the most liberal standards—a strikingly corrupt old person, yet he still has this word "Pope" attached to him. And from this quite meaningless circumstance I fear some degree of . . .

RICH (*Pleased, waving his cup*) . . . Administrative inconvenience.

CROMWELL (*Nodding as to a word-perfect pupil*) Just so. (*Deadpan*) This goblet that he gave you, how much was it worth? (RICH *looks down. Quite gently*) Come along, Rich, he gave you a silver goblet. How much did you get for it?

RICH Fifty shillings.

CROMWELL Could you take me to the shop?

RICH Yes.

CROMWELL Where did he get it? (*No reply.* RICH *puts the cup down*) It was a gift from a litigant, a woman, wasn't it?

RICH Yes.

CROMWELL Which court? Chancery? (*Takes the bottle; re-*

strains RICH *from filling his glass*) No, don't get drunk. In which court was this litigant's case?

RICH   Court of Requests.

CROMWELL (*Grunts, his face abstracted. Becoming aware of* RICH's *regard, he smiles*)   There, that wasn't too painful, was it?

RICH (*Laughing a little and a little rueful*)   No!

CROMWELL (*Spreading his hands*)   That's all there is. And you'll find it easier next time.

RICH (*Looks up briefly, unhappily*)   What application do they have, these tidbits of information you collect?

CROMWELL   None at all, usually.

RICH (*Stubbornly, not looking up*)   But sometimes.

CROMWELL   Well, there *are* these men—you know—"upright," "steadfast," men who want themselves to be the constant factor in the situation; which, of course, they can't be. The situation rolls forward in any case.

RICH (*Still stubbornly*)   So what happens?

CROMWELL (*Not liking his tone, coldly*)   If they've any sense they get out of its way.

RICH   What if they haven't any sense?

CROMWELL (*Still coldly*) What, none at all? Well, then they're only fit for Heaven. But Sir Thomas has plenty of sense; he could be frightened.

RICH (*Looks up, his face nasty*) Don't forget he's an innocent, Master Cromwell.

CROMWELL I think we'll finish there for tonight. After all, he *is* the Lord Chancellor.
(*Going*)

RICH You wouldn't find him easy to frighten! (CROMWELL *exits. He calls after him*) You've mistaken your man this time! He doesn't know how to be frightened!

CROMWELL (*Returning.* RICH *rises at his approach*) Doesn't know how to be frightened? Why, then he never put his hand in a candle . . . Did he?
(*And seizing* RICH *by the wrist he holds his hand in the candle flame*)

RICH (*Screeches and darts back, hugging his hand in his armpit, regarding* CROMWELL *with horror*) You enjoyed that!
(CROMWELL'S *downturned face is amazed. Triumphantly*)
You enjoyed it!

Curtain

ACT TWO

The scene is as for start of Act One. When the curtain rises the stage is in darkness save for a spot, in which stands the COMMON MAN. *He carries the book, a place marked by his finger, and wears his spectacles.*

COMMON MAN   The interval started early in the year 1530 and it's now the middle of May, 1532. (*Explanatory*) Two years. During that time a lot of water's flowed under the bridge, and one of the things that have come floating along on it is . . . (*Reads*) "The Church of England, that finest flower of our Island genius for compromise; that system, peculiar to these shores, the despair of foreign observers, which deflects the torrents of religious passion down the canals of moderation." That's very well put. (*Returns to the book, approvingly*) "Typically, this great effect was achieved not by bloodshed but by simple Act of Parliament. Only an unhappy few were found to set themselves against the current of their times, and in so doing to court disaster. For we are dealing with an age less fastidious than our own. Imprisonment without trial, and even examination under torture, were common practice."
(*Lights rise to show* MORE, *seated, and* ROPER, *standing. Exit* COMMON MAN. ROPER *is dressed in black and wears a cross. He commences to walk up and down, watched by* MORE. *A pause*)

MORE   Must you wear those clothes, Will?

ROPER   Yes, I must.

MORE   Why?

81

ROPER The time has come for decent men to declare their allegiance!

MORE And what allegiance are those designed to express?

ROPER My allegiance to the Church.

MORE Well, you *look* like a Spaniard.

ROPER All credit to Spain then!

MORE You wouldn't last six months in Spain. You'd have been burned alive in Spain, during your heretic period.

ROPER I suppose you have the right to remind me of it. (*Points accusingly*) That chain of office that *you* wear is a degradation!

MORE (*Glances down at it*) I've told you. If the bishops in Convocation submitted this morning, I'll take it off . . . It's no degradation. Great men have worn this.

ROPER When d'you expect to hear from the bishops?

MORE About now. I was promised an immediate message.

ROPER (*Recommences pacing*) I don't see what difference Convocation can make. The Church is already a wing of the Palace, is it not? The King is already its "Supreme Head"! Is he not?

MORE No.

ROPER (*Startled*) You are denying the Act of Supremacy!

MORE No, I'm not; the Act states that the King—

ROPER —is Supreme Head of the Church in England.

MORE Supreme Head of the Church in England— (*Underlin-ing the words*) "so far as the law of God allows." How far the law of God does allow it remains a matter of opinion, since the Act doesn't state it.

ROPER A legal quibble.

MORE Call it what you like, it's there, thank God.

ROPER Very well; in your opinion how far does the law of God allow this?

MORE I'll keep my opinion to myself, Will.

ROPER Yes? I'll tell you mine—

MORE Don't! If your opinion's what I think it is, it's High Treason, Roper! (*Enter* MARGARET *above, unseen*) Will you remember you've a wife now! And may have children!

MARGARET Why must he remember that?

ROPER To keep myself "discreet."

MARGARET (*Smiling*) Then I'd rather you forgot it.

MORE (*Unsmiling*)   You are either idiots, or children.
(*Enter* CHAPUYS, *above*)

CHAPUYS (*Very sonorously*)   Or saints, my lord!

MARGARET   Oh, Father, Signor Chapuys has come to see you.

MORE (*Rising*)   Your Excellency.

CHAPUYS (*Strikes pose with* MARGARET *and* ROPER)   Or saints,
my lord; or saints.

MORE (*Grins maliciously at* ROPER)   That's it of course—
saints! Roper—turn your head a bit—yes, I think I do detect a
faint radiance. (*Reproachfully*) You should have told us,
Will.

CHAPUYS   Come come, my lord; you too at this time are not
free from some suspicion of saintliness.

MORE (*Quietly*)   I don't like the sound of that, Your Excellency. What do you require of *me*? What, Your Excellency?

CHAPUYS (*Awkward beneath his sudden keen regard*)   May
I not come simply to pay my respects to the English Socrates—as I see your angelic friend Erasmus calls you.

MORE (*Wrinkles nose*)   Yes, I'll think of something presently
to call Erasmus. (*Checks*) Socrates! I've no taste for hem-
lock, Your Excellency, if that's what you require.

CHAPUYS (*With a display of horror*)   Heaven forbid!

MORE (*Dryly*) Amen.

CHAPUYS (*Spreads hands*) Must I require anything? (*Sonorously*) After all, we are brothers in Christ, you and I!

MORE A characteristic we share with the rest of humanity. You live in Cheapside, Signor? To make contact with a brother in Christ you have only to open your window and empty a chamberpot. There was no need to come to Chelsea. (CHAPUYS *titters nervously. Coldly*) William. The Spanish Ambassador is here on business. Would you mind?
(ROPER *and* MARGARET *begin to go*)

CHAPUYS (*Rising, unreal protestations*) Oh no! I protest!

MORE He is clearly here on business.

CHAPUYS No; but really, I protest! (*It is no more than token: when* ROPER *and* MARGARET *reach head of stairs he calls*) Dominus vobiscum filii mei!

ROPER (*Pompously*) Et cum spiritu tuo, excellencis!
(*Exit* ROPER *and* MARGARET)

CHAPUYS (*Approaching* MORE, *thrillingly*) And how much longer shall we hear that holy language in these shores?

MORE (*Alert, poker-faced*) 'Tisn't "holy," Your Excellency; just old.
(CHAPUYS *sits with the air of one getting down to brass tacks*)

CHAPUYS My lord, I cannot believe you will allow yourself to be associated with the recent actions of King Henry! In respect of Queen Catherine.

MORE Subjects are associated with the actions of Kings willy-nilly.

CHAPUYS The Lord Chancellor is not an ordinary subject. He bears responsibility (*He lets the word sink in;* MORE *shifts*) for what is done.

MORE (*Agitation begins to show through*) Have you considered that what has been done badly, might have been done worse, with a different Chancellor.

CHAPUYS (*Mounting confidence, as* MORE'S *attention is caught*) Believe me, Sir Thomas, your influence in these policies has been much searched for, and where it has been found it has been praised—*but* . . . There comes a point, does there not? . . .

MORE Yes. (*Agitated*) There does come such a point.

CHAPUYS When the sufferings of one unfortunate lady swell to an open attack on the religion of an entire country that point has been passed. Beyond that point, Sir Thomas, one is not merely "compromised," one is in truth corrupted.

MORE (*Stares at him*) What do you want?

CHAPUYS Rumor has it that if the Church in Convocation has submitted to the King, you will resign.

86

MORE (*Looks down and regains composure*) I see. (*Suavely*) Supposing rumor to be right. Would you approve of that?

CHAPUYS Approve, applaud, admire.

MORE (*Still looking down*) Why?

CHAPUYS Because it would show one man—and that man known to be temperate—unable to go further with this wickedness.

MORE And that man known to be Chancellor of England too.

CHAPUYS Believe me, my lord, such a signal would be seen—

MORE "Signal"?

CHAPUYS Yes, my lord; it would be seen and understood.

MORE (*Now positively silky*) By whom?

CHAPUYS By half of your fellow countrymen! (*Now MORE looks up sharply*) Sir Thomas, I have just returned from Yorkshire and Northumberland, where I have made a tour.

MORE (*Softly*) Have you indeed?

CHAPUYS Things are very different there, my lord. There they are ready.

MORE For what?

CHAPUYS Resistance!

MORE (*Softly, as before*) Resistance by what means? (*Suddenly his agitation must find expression, if only physical. He is galvanized from his seat and as he suddenly stops, with his back to* CHAPUYS, MORE'S *face is electrically alert.* CHAPUYS *hears the excitement in:*) By force of arms?

CHAPUYS (*Almost sure the fish is hooked, leaning forward but playing it cool*) We are adjured by St. Paul to don the arms of God when the occasion warrants.

MORE Metaphorical arms. The breastplate of righteousness and the helmet of salvation. Do you mean a metaphorical resistance?
(*Indignation and fear make his voice vibrate with the excitement of enthusiasm*)

CHAPUYS (*Intones*) "He shall flee the *iron* weapons, and the bow of steel shall strike him through."

MORE (*There is a pause while his agile mind scans the full frightening implications of this for himself; it is almost with a start of recollection that he remembers to answer* CHAPUYS *at all*) I see.
(*Enter* ROPER, *above, excited*)

ROPER Sir Thomas! (MORE *looks up angrily*) Excuse me, sir— (*Indicates off*) His Grace the Duke of Norfolk— (MORE *and* CHAPUYS *rise.* ROPER *excitedly descends*) It's all over, sir, they've—
(*Enter* NORFOLK *above,* ALICE *and* MARGARET, *below*)

NORFOLK   One moment, Roper, I'll do this! Thomas— (*Sees* CHAPUYS) Oh.
(*He stares at* CHAPUYS *hostilely*)

CHAPUYS   I was on the point of leaving, Your Grace. Just a personal call. I have been trying . . . er, to borrow a book . . . but without success—you're sure you have no copy, my lord? Then I'll leave you. (*Bowing*) Gentlemen, ladies.
(*Going up the stairs, he stops unnoticed as* ROPER *speaks*)

ROPER   Sir Thomas—

NORFOLK   I'll do it, Roper! Convocation's knuckled under, Thomas. They're to pay a fine of a hundred thousand pounds. And . . . we've severed the connection with Rome.

MORE (*Smiling bitterly*)   "The connection with Rome" is nice. (*Bitterly*) "The connection with Rome."

ROPER (*Addressing Norfolk, but looking at* MORE)   Your Grace, this is quite certain, is it?

NORFOLK   Yes. (MORE *puts his hand to his chain.* CHAPUYS *exits. All turn*) Funny company, Thomas?

MORE   It's quite unintentional. He doesn't mean to be funny. (*He fumbles with the chain*) Help me with this.

NORFOLK   Not I.

ROPER (*Takes a step forward. Then, subdued*)   Shall I, sir?

MORE   No thank you, Will. Alice?

ALICE   Hell's fire—God's Blood and Body, *no!* Sun and moon, Master More, you're taken for a wise man! Is this wisdom— to betray your ability, abandon practice, forget your station and your duty to your kin and behave like a printed book!

MORE (*Listens gravely; then*)   Margaret, will you?

MARGARET   If you want.

MORE   There's my clever girl.
  (*She takes it from his neck*)

NORFOLK   Well, Thomas, why? Make me understand—be- cause I'll tell you now, from where I stand, this looks like cowardice!

MORE (*Excited and angry*)   All right I will—this isn't "Refor- mation," this is war against the Church! . . . (*Indignant*) Our King, Norfolk, has declared war on the Pope—because the Pope will not declare that our Queen is not his wife.

NORFOLK   And is she?

MORE (*With cunning*)   I'll answer that question for one per- son only, the King. Aye, and that in private too.

NORFOLK (*Contemptuously*)   Man, you're cautious.

MORE   Yes, cautious. I'm not one of your hawks.

NORFOLK (*Walks away and turns*) All right—we're at war with the Pope! The Pope's a Prince, isn't he?

MORE He is.

NORFOLK And a bad one?

MORE Bad enough. But the theory is that he's also the Vicar of God, the descendant of St. Peter, our only link with Christ.

NORFOLK (*Sneering*) A tenuous link.

MORE Oh, tenuous indeed.

NORFOLK (*To the others*) Does this make sense? (*No reply; they look at* MORE) You'll forfeit all you've got—which includes the respect of your country—for a theory?

MORE (*Hotly*) The Apostolic Succession of the Pope is— (*Stops; interested*) . . . Why, it's a theory, yes; you can't see it; can't touch it; it's a theory. (*To* NORFOLK, *very rapidly but calmly*) But what matters to me is not whether it's true or not but that I believe it to be true, or rather, not that I *believe* it, but that *I* believe it . . . I trust I make myself obscure?

NORFOLK Perfectly.

MORE That's good. Obscurity's what I have need of now.

NORFOLK Thomas. This isn't Spain, you know.

MORE (*Looks at him, takes him aside; in a lowered voice*) Have I your word that what we say here is between us and has no existence beyond these walls?

NORFOLK (*Impatient*) Very well.

MORE (*Almost whispering*) And if the King should command you to repeat what I have said?

NORFOLK I should keep my word to you!

MORE Then what has become of your oath of obedience to the King?

NORFOLK (*Indignant*) You lay traps for me!

MORE (*Now grown calm*) No, I show you the times.

NORFOLK Why do you insult me with these lawyer's tricks?

MORE Because I am afraid.

NORFOLK And here's your answer. The King accepts your resignation very sadly; he is mindful of your goodness and past loyalty, and in any matter concerning your honor and welfare he will be your good lord. So much for your fear.

MORE (*Flatly*) You will convey my humble gratitude.

NORFOLK I will. Good day, Alice. (*Going*) I'd rather deal with you than your husband.

MORE (*Complete change of tone; briskly professional*) Oh, Howard! (*He stops him*) Signor Chapuys tells me he's just made a "tour" of the North Country. He thinks we shall have trouble there. So do I.

NORFOLK (*Stolid*) Yes? What kind of trouble?

MORE The Church—the old Church, not the new Church—is very strong up there. I'm serious, Howard, keep an eye on the border this next spring; and bear in mind the Old Alliance.

NORFOLK (*Looks at him*) We will. We do . . . As for the Spaniard, Thomas, it'll perhaps relieve your mind to know that one of Secretary Cromwell's agents made the tour with him.

MORE Oh. (*A flash of jealousy*) Of course if Master Cromwell has matters in hand—

NORFOLK He has.

MORE Yes, I can imagine.

NORFOLK But thanks for the information. (*Going upstairs*) It's good to know you still have . . . some vestige of patriotism.

MORE (*Angrily*) That's a remarkably stupid observation, Norfolk!
(NORFOLK *exits*)

ALICE So there's an end of you. What will you do now—sit by the fire and make goslings in the ash?

93

MORE Not at all, Alice, I expect I'll write a bit. (*He woos them with unhappy cheerfulness*) I'll write, I'll read, I'll think. I think I'll learn to fish! I'll play with my grandchildren—when son Roper's done his duty. (*Eagerly*) Alice, shall I teach you to read?

ALICE No, by God!

MORE Son Roper, *you're* pleased with me I hope?

ROPER (*Goes to him; moved*) Sir, you've made a noble gesture.

MORE (*Blankly*) A gesture? (*Eagerly*) It wasn't possible to continue, Will. I was not *able* to continue. I would have if I could! I make no gesture! (*Apprehensive, looks after* NORFOLK) My God, I hope it's understood I make no gesture! (*He turns back to them*) Alice, you don't think I would do this to you for a gesture! *That's* a gesture! (*Thumbs his nose*) *That's* a gesture! (*Jerks up two fingers*) I'm no street acrobat to make gestures! I'm practical!

ROPER You belittle yourself, sir, this was not practical; (*Resonantly*) this was moral!

MORE Oh, now I understand you, Will. Morality's *not* practical. Morality's a gesture. A complicated gesture learned from books—that's what you say, Alice, isn't it? . . . And you, Meg?

MARGARET It *is*, for most of us, Father.

MORE Oh no, if you're going to plead humility! Oh, you're cruel. I have a cruel family.

ALICE Yes, you can fit the cap on anyone you want, I know that well enough. If there's cruelty in this house, I know where to look for it.

MARGARET No, Mother!

ALICE Oh, you'd walk on the bottom of the sea and think yourself a crab if he suggested it! (*To* ROPER) And you! You'd dance him to the Tower— You'd dance him to the block! Like David with a harp! Scattering hymn books in his path! (*To* MORE) Poor silly man, d'you think they'll *leave* you here to learn to fish?

MORE (*Straight at her*) If we govern our tongues they will! Now listen, I have a word to say about that. I have made no statement. I've resigned, that's *all*. On the King's Supremacy, the King's divorce which he'll now grant himself, the marriage he'll then make—have you heard me make a statement?

ALICE No—and if I'm to lose my rank and fall to housekeeping I want to know the reason; so make a statement now.

MORE No— (ALICE *exhibits indignation*) Alice, it's a point of law! Accept it from me, Alice, that in silence is my safety under the law, but my silence must be absolute, it must extend to you.

ALICE In short you don't trust us!

MORE A man would need to be half-witted not to trust you— but— (*Impatiently*) Look— (*He advances on her*) I'm the Lord Chief Justice, I'm Cromwell, I'm the King's Head Jailer

—and I take your hand (*He does so*) and I clamp it on the Bible, on the Blessed Cross (*Clamps her hand on his closed fist*) and I say: "Woman, has your husband made a statement on these matters?" Now—on peril of your soul remember—what's your answer?

ALICE No.

MORE And so it must remain. (*He looks around at their grave faces*) Oh, it's only a life line, we shan't have to use it but it's comforting to have. No, no, when they find I'm silent they'll ask nothing better than to leave me silent; you'll see. (*Enter* STEWARD)

STEWARD Sir, the household's in the kitchen. They want to know what's happened.

MORE Oh. Yes. We must speak to them. Alice, they'll mostly have to go, my dear. (*To* STEWARD) But not before we've found them places.

ALICE We can't find places for them all!

MORE Yes, we can; yes, we can. Tell them so.

ALICE God's death, it comes on us quickly . . .
(*Exit* ALICE, MARGARET *with the chain, and* ROPER)

MORE What about you, Matthew? It'll be a smaller household now, and for you I'm afraid, a smaller wage. Will you stay?

STEWARD Don't see how I could then, sir.

MORE You're a single man.

STEWARD (*Awkwardly*) Well, yes, sir, but I mean I've got my own—

MORE (*Quickly*) Quite right, why should you? . . . I shall miss you, Matthew.

STEWARD (*With man-to-man jocosity*) No-o-o. You never had much time for me, sir. You see through *me*, sir, I know that. (*He almost winks*)

MORE (*Gently insists*) I shall miss you, Matthew; I shall miss you.
(*Exit* MORE. STEWARD *snatches off his hat and hurls it to the floor*)

STEWARD Now, damn me, isn't that them all over! (*He broods, face downturned*) Miss? . . . He . . . Miss? . . . Miss me? . . . What's *in* me for *him* to miss? . . . (*Suddenly he cries out like one who sees a danger at his very feet*) Wo-AH! (*Chuckling*) We-e-eyup! (*To audience*) I nearly fell for it. (*He walks away*) "Matthew, will you kindly take a cut in your wages?" "No, Sir Thomas, I will not." That's it and (*Fiercely*) that's all of it! (*Falls to thought again. Resentfully*) All right, so he's down on his luck! I'm sorry. I don't mind saying that: I'm sorry! Bad luck! If I'd any good luck to spare he could have some. I wish we could *all* have good luck, *all* the time! I wish we had wings! I wish rain-

97

water was beer! But it isn't! . . . And what with not having wings but walking—on two flat feet; and good luck and bad luck being just exactly even stevens; and rain being water— don't you complicate the job by putting things in me for me to miss! (*He takes off his steward's coat, picks up his hat; draws the curtain to the alcove. Chuckling*) I did, you know. I nearly fell for it.

(*Exit* COMMON MAN. NORFOLK *and* CROMWELL *enter to alcove*)

NORFOLK   But he makes no noise, Mr. Secretary; he's silent, why not leave him silent?

CROMWELL (*Patiently*)   Not being a man of letters, Your Grace, you perhaps don't realize the extent of his reputation. This "silence" of his is bellowing up and down Europe! Now may I recapitulate: He reported the Spaniard's conversation to you, informed on the Spaniard's tour of the North Country, warned against a possible rebellion there.

NORFOLK   He did!

CROMWELL   We may say, then, that he showed himself hostile to the hopes of Spain.

NORFOLK   That's what I *say!*

CROMWELL (*Patiently*)   Bear with me, Your Grace. Now if he opposes Spain, he supports us. Well, surely that follows? (*Sarcastically*) Or do you see some third alternative?

NORFOLK   No no, that's the line-up all right. And I may say Thomas More—

CROMWELL Thomas More will line up on the right side.

NORFOLK Yes! Crank he may be, traitor he is not.

CROMWELL (*Spreading his hands*) And with a little pressure, he can be got to say so. And that's all we need—a brief declaration of his loyalty to the present administration.

NORFOLK I still say let sleeping dogs lie.

CROMWELL (*Heavily*) The King does not agree with you.

NORFOLK (*Glances at him, flickers, but then rallies*) What kind of "pressure" d'you think you can bring to bear?

CROMWELL I have evidence that Sir Thomas, during the period of his judicature, accepted bribes.

NORFOLK (*Incredulous*) What! Goddammit, he was the only judge since Cato who *didn't* accept bribes! When was there last a Chancellor whose possessions after three years in office totaled one hundred pounds and a gold chain.

CROMWELL (*Rings hand bell and calls*) Richard! It is, as you imply, common practice, but a practice may be common and remain an offense; this offense could send a man to the Tower.

NORFOLK (*Contemptuously*) I don't believe it.
(*Enter a* WOMAN *and* RICH, *who motions her to remain and approaches the table, where* CROMWELL *indicates a seat.* RICH *has acquired self-importance.*)

CROMWELL Ah, Richard. You know His Grace, of course.

RICH (*Respectful affability*) Indeed yes, we're *old* friends.

NORFOLK (*Savage snub*) Used to look after my books or something, didn't you?

CROMWELL (*Clicks his fingers at* WOMAN) Come here. This woman's name is Catherine Anger; she comes from Lincoln. And she put a case in the Court of Requests in—
(*Consults a paper*)

WOMAN A property case, it was.

CROMWELL Be quiet. A property case in the Court of Requests in April, 1526.

WOMAN And got a wicked false judgment!

CROMWELL And got an impeccably correct judgment from our friend Sir Thomas.

WOMAN No, sir, it was not!

CROMWELL We're not concerned with the judgment but the gift you gave the judge. Tell this gentleman about that. The judgment, for what it's worth, was the right one.

WOMAN No, sir! (CROMWELL *looks at her; she hastily addresses* NORFOLK) I sent him a cup, sir, an Italian silver cup I bought in Lincoln for a hundred shillings.

NORFOLK   Did Sir Thomas accept this cup?

WOMAN   I sent it.

CROMWELL   He did accept it, we can corroborate that. You
can go. (*She opens her mouth*) Go!
(*Exit* WOMAN)

NORFOLK (*Scornfully*)   Is that your witness?

CROMWELL   No; by an odd coincidence this cup later came
into the hands of Master Rich here.

NORFOLK   How?

RICH   He gave it to me.

NORFOLK (*Brutally*)   Can you corroborate that?

CROMWELL   I have a fellow outside who can; he was More's
steward at that time. Shall I call him?

NORFOLK   Don't bother, I know him. When did Thomas give
you this thing?

RICH   I don't exactly remember.

NORFOLK   Well, make an effort. Wait! I can tell you! I can
tell you—it was that spring—it was that night we were there
together. You had a cup with you when we left; was that it?
(RICH *looks to* CROMWELL *for guidance but gets none*)

RICH   It may have been.

NORFOLK   Did he often give you cups?

RICH   I don't suppose so, Your Grace.

NORFOLK   That was it then. (*New realization*) And it was April! The April of twenty-six. The very month that cow first put her case before him! (*Triumphantly*) In other words, the moment he knew it was a bribe, he got rid of it.

CROMWELL (*Nodding judicially*)   The facts will bear that interpretation, I suppose.

NORFOLK   Oh, this is a horse that won't run, Master Secretary.

CROMWELL   Just a trial canter, Your Grace. We'll find something better.

NORFOLK (*Between bullying and pleading*)   Look here, Cromwell, I want no part of this.

CROMWELL   You have no choice.

NORFOLK   What's that you say?

CROMWELL   The King particularly wishes you to be active in the matter.

NORFOLK (*Winded*)   He has not told me that.

CROMWELL (*Politely*)   Indeed? He told me.

NORFOLK But *why?*

CROMWELL We feel that, since you are known to have been a friend of More's, your participation will show that there is nothing in the nature of a "persecution," but only the strict processes of law. As indeed you've just demonstrated. I'll tell the King of your loyalty to your friend. If you like, I'll tell him that you "want no part of it," too.

NORFOLK (*Furious*) Are you threatening me, Cromwell?

CROMWELL My *dear* Norfolk . . . This isn't Spain.
(NORFOLK *stares, turns abruptly and exits.* CROMWELL *turns a look of glacial coldness upon* RICH)

RICH I'm sorry, Secretary, I'd forgotten he was there that night.

CROMWELL (*Scrutinizes him dispassionately; then*) You must try to remember these things.

RICH Secretary, I'm sincerely—

CROMWELL (*Dismisses the topic with a wave and turns to look after* NORFOLK) Not such a fool as he looks, the Duke.

RICH (*Civil Service simper*) That would hardly be possible, Secretary.

CROMWELL (*Straightening his papers, briskly*) Sir Thomas is going to be a slippery fish, Richard; we need a net with a finer mesh.

RICH   Yes, Secretary?

CROMWELL   We'll weave one for him, shall we, you and I?

RICH (*Uncertainly*)   I'm only anxious to do what is correct, Secretary.

CROMWELL (*Smiling at him*)   Yes, Richard, I know. (*Straight-faced*) You're absolutely right, it must be done by law. It's just a matter of finding the right law. Or making one. Bring my papers, will you?
(*Exit* CROMWELL. *Enter* STEWARD)

STEWARD   Could we have a word now, sir?

RICH   We don't require you after all, Matthew.

STEWARD   No, sir, but about . . .

RICH   Oh yes. . . . Well, I begin to need a steward, certainly; my household is expanding . . . (*Sharply*) But as I remember, Matthew, your attitude to me was sometimes—disrespectful!
(*The last word is shrill*)

STEWARD (*With humble dignity*)   Oh. Oh, I must contradict you there, sir; that's your imagination. In those days, sir, you still had your way to make. And a gentleman in that position often imagines these things. Then when he's reached his proper level, sir, he stops thinking about them. (*As if offering tangible proof*) Well—I don't think you find people "disrespectful" nowadays, do you, sir?

RICH   There may be something in that. Bring my papers. (*Going, he turns at the exit and anxiously scans* STEWARD's *face for signs of impudence*) I'll permit no breath of insolence!

STEWARD (*The very idea is shocking*)   I should hope not, sir. (*Exit* RICH) Oh, I can manage this one! He's just my size! (*Lighting changes so that the set looks drab and chilly*) Sir Thomas More's again. Gone down a bit.
(*Exit* COMMON MAN. *Enter* CHAPUYS *and* ATTENDANT, *cloaked.* ALICE *enters above wearing a big coarse apron over her dress*)

ALICE   My husband is coming down, Your Excellency.

CHAPUYS   Thank you, madam.

ALICE   And I beg you to be gone before he does!

CHAPUYS (*Patiently*)   Madam, I have a Royal Commission to perform.

ALICE   Aye. You said so.
(ALICE *exits*)

CHAPUYS   For sheer barbarity, commend me to a good-hearted Englishwoman of a certain class. . . .
(*Wraps cloak about him*)

ATTENDANT   It's very cold, Excellency.

CHAPUYS   I remember when these rooms were warm enough.

ATTENDANT (*Looking about*) "Thus it is to incur the enmity of a King."

CHAPUYS A heretic King. (*Looking about*) Yes, Sir Thomas is a good man.

ATTENDANT Yes, Excellency, I like Sir Thomas very much.

CHAPUYS Carefully, carefully.

ATTENDANT It *is* uncomfortable dealing with him, isn't it?

CHAPUYS (*Smilingly patronizing*) Goodness can be a difficulty.

ATTENDANT (*Somewhat shocked*) Excellency?

CHAPUYS (*Recovers instantly his official gravity*) In the long run, of course, *all* good men everywhere are allies of Spain. No good man cannot be, and no man who is not can be good . . .

ATTENDANT Then he is really for us.

CHAPUYS (*Still graciously instructing*) He is opposed to Cromwell, is he not?

ATTENDANT (*Smiling back*) Oh, yes, Excellency.

CHAPUYS (*As a genteel card player, primly triumphant, produces the ace of trumps*) If he's opposed to Cromwell, he's for us. (*No answer; a little more sharply*) There's no third alternative?

ATTENDANT   I suppose not, Excellency.

CHAPUYS (*Rides him down, tried beyond all bearing*)   Oh—I
wish your mother had chosen some other career for you.
You've no political sense whatever! (*Enter* MORE) Sir
Thomas! (*Goes to him, solemnly and affectionately places
hands on his shoulders, gazing into his eyes*) Ah, Sir
Thomas, in a better state this threadbare stuff will meta-
morphose into shining garments, these dank walls to walls
of pearl, this cold light to perpetual sunshine.
(*He bends upon* MORE *a melancholy look of admiration*)

MORE (*As yet quite friendly, smiles quizzically*)   It sounds not
unlike Madrid . . . ?

CHAPUYS (*Throws up his hands delightedly*)   Even in times
like this, even now, a pleasure to converse with you.

MORE (*Chuckles a little, takes* CHAPUYS *by the wrist, waggles
it a little and then releases it as though to indicate that
pleasantries must now end*)   Is this another "personal" visit,
Chapuys, or is it official?

CHAPUYS   It falls between the two, Sir Thomas.

MORE (*Reaching the bottom of stairs*)   Official then.

CHAPUYS   No, I have a personal letter for you.

MORE   From whom?

CHAPUYS   My master, the King of Spain. (MORE *puts his hands
behind his back*) You will take it?

MORE   I will not lay a finger on it.

CHAPUYS   It is in no way an affair of State. It expresses my master's admiration for the stand which you and Bishop Fisher of Rochester have taken over the so-called divorce of Queen Catherine.

MORE   I have taken no stand!

CHAPUYS   But your views, Sir Thomas, are well known—

MORE   My views are much guessed at. (*Irritably*) Oh come, sir, could you undertake to convince (*Grimly*) King Harry that this letter is "in no way an affair of State?"

CHAPUYS   My dear Sir Thomas, I have taken extreme precautions. I came here very much incognito. (*A self-indulgent chuckle*) Very nearly in disguise.

MORE   You misunderstand me. It is not a matter of your precautions but my duty, which would be to take this letter immediately to the King.

CHAPUYS (*Flabbergasted*)   But, Sir Thomas, your views—

MORE (*With the heat of* fear *behind it*)   Are well known you say. It seems my loyalty to my King is less so!

CHAPUYS (*Glibly*)   "Render unto Caesar the things which *are* Caesar's— (*He raises a reproving finger*) But unto God—"

MORE   Stop! (*He walks about, suppressing his agitation, and*

then as one who excuses a display of bad manners) Holy
writ is holy, Excellency.
(Enter MARGARET *bearing before her a huge bundle of
bracken. The entry of the bracken affords him a further opportunity to collect himself)*

MARGARET   Look, Father! *(She dumps it)* Will's getting more.

MORE   Oh, well done! *(This is not whimsy; they're cold and
their interest in fuel is serious)* Is it dry? *(He feels it ex-
pertly)* Oh it *is.* *(Sees* CHAPUYS *staring; laughs)* It's bracken,
Your Excellency. We burn it. *(Enter* ALICE*)* Alice, look at
this.

ALICE *(Eying* CHAPUYS*)*   Aye.

MORE *(Crossing to* CHAPUYS*)*   May I? *(Takes the letter to
ALICE and* MARGARET*)* This is a letter from the King of
Spain; I want you to see it's not been opened. I have de-
clined it. You see the seal has not been broken? *(Returning
it to* CHAPUYS*)* I wish I could ask you to stay, Your Excellency—the bracken fire is a luxury.

CHAPUYS *(With a cold smile)*   One I must forgo. *(Aside
to* ATTENDANT*)* Come. *(Crosses to exit, pauses)* May I say
I am sure my master's admiration will not be diminished.
(Bows, noncommittally) Ladies.

MORE   I'm gratified.

CHAPUYS *(Bows to them, the ladies curtsy)*   The man's utterly
unreliable.
(Exit CHAPUYS *and* ATTENDANT*)*

ALICE (*After a little silence kicks the bracken*)   "Luxury"!
(*She sits wearily on the bundle*)

MORE   Well, it's a luxury while it lasts . . . There's not
much sport in it for you, is there? (*She neither answers nor
looks at him from the depths of her fatigue. After a moment's
hesitation he braces himself*) Alice, the money from the
bishops. I can't take it. I wish—oh, heaven, how I wish I
could! But I can't.

ALICE (*As one who has ceased to expect anything*)   I didn't
think you would.

MORE (*Reproachfully*)   Alice, there *are* reasons.

ALICE   We couldn't come so deep into your confidence as to
know these reasons why a man in poverty can't take four
thousand pounds?

MORE (*Gently but very firmly*)   Alice, this isn't poverty.

ALICE   D'you know what we shall eat tonight?

MORE (*Trying for a smile*)   Yes, parsnips.

ALICE   Yes, parsnips and stinking mutton! (*Straight at him*)
For a knight's lady!

MORE (*Pleading*)   But at the worst, we could be beggars, and
still keep company, and be merry together!

ALICE (*Bitterly*)   Merry!

MORE (*Sternly*) Aye, merry!

MARGARET (*Her arm about her mother's waist*) I think you should take that money.

MORE Oh, don't you see? (*He sits by them*) If I'm paid by the Church for my writings—

ALICE This had nothing to do with your writings! This was charity pure and simple! Collected from the clergy high and low!

MORE It would *appear* as payment.

ALICE You're not a man who deals in appearances!

MORE (*Fervently*) Oh, am I not though. . . . (*Calmly*) If the King takes this matter any further, with me or with the Church, it will be very bad, if I even appear to have been in the pay of the Church.

ALICE (*Sharply*) Bad?

MORE If you will have it, dangerous.

MARGARET But you don't write against the King.

MORE (*Rises*) I write! And that's enough in times like these!

ALICE You said there *was* no danger!

MORE I don't think there is! And I don't want there to be!
(*Enter* ROPER *carrying a sickle*)

ROPER (*Steadily*) There's a gentleman here from Hampton Court. You are to go before Secretary Cromwell. To answer certain charges.
(ALICE *rises and* MARGARET, *appalled, turns to* MORE)

MORE (*After a silence, rubs his nose*) Well, that's all right. We expected that. (*He is not very convincing*) When?

ROPER Now.

ALICE (*Exhibits distress*) Ah—

MORE Alice, that means nothing; that's just technique . . . Well, I suppose "now" means now.
(*Lighting changes, darkness gathering on the others, leaving* MORE *isolated in the light*)

MARGARET Can I come with you?

MORE Why? No. I'll be back for dinner. I'll bring Cromwell to dinner, shall I? It'd serve him right.

MARGARET Oh, Father, don't be witty!

MORE Why not? Wit's what's in question.

ROPER (*Quietly*) While we are witty, the Devil may enter us unawares.

MORE He's not the Devil, son Roper, he's a lawyer! And **my** case is watertight!

ALICE They say he's a very penetrating lawyer.

MORE What, Cromwell? Pooh, he's a pragmatist—and that's the only resemblance he has to the Devil, son Roper; a pragmatist, the merest plumber.
(*Exit* ALICE, MARGARET, ROPER, *in darkness. Lights come up. Enter* CROMWELL, *bustling, carrying a file of papers*)

CROMWELL I'm sorry to invite you here at such short notice, Sir Thomas; good of you to come. (*Draws back curtain from alcove, revealing* RICH *seated at a table, with writing materials*) Will you take a seat? I think you know Master Rich?

MORE Indeed yes, we're old friends. That's a nice gown you have, Richard.

CROMWELL Master Rich will make a record of our conversation.

MORE Good of you to tell me, Master Secretary.

CROMWELL (*Laughs appreciatively; then*) Believe me, Sir Thomas—no, that's asking too much—but let me tell you all the same, you have no more sincere admirer than myself. (RICH *begins to scribble*) Not yet, Rich, not yet.
(*Invites* MORE *to join him in laughing at* RICH)

MORE If I might hear the charges?

CROMWELL Charges?

MORE I understand there are certain charges.

CROMWELL   Some abiguities of behavior I should like to clarify—hardly "charges."

MORE   Make a note of that will you, Master Rich? There are no charges.

CROMWELL (*Laughing and shaking head*)   Sir Thomas, Sir Thomas . . . You know it amazes me that you, who were once so effective *in* the world and are now so *much* retired from it, should be opposing yourself to the whole movement of the times?
(*He ends on a note of interrogation*)

MORE (*Nods*)   It amazes me too.

CROMWELL (*Picks up and drops a paper; sadly*)   The King is not pleased with you.

MORE   I am grieved.

CROMWELL   Yet do you know that even now, if you could bring yourself to agree with the Universities, the Bishops, and the Parliament of this realm, there is no honor which the King would be likely to deny you?

MORE (*Stonily*)   I am well acquainted with His Grace's generosity.

CROMWELL (*Coldly*)   Very well. (*Consults the paper*) You have heard of the so-called Holy Maid of Kent—who was executed for prophesying against the King?

114

MORE   Yes, I knew the poor woman.

CROMWELL (*Quickly*)   You sympathize with her?

MORE   She was ignorant and misguided; she was a bit mad, I think. And she has paid for her folly. Naturally I sympathize with her.

CROMWELL (*Grunts*)   You admit meeting her. You met her—and yet you did not warn His Majesty of her treason. How was that?

MORE   She spoke no treason. Our conversation was not political.

CROMWELL   My dear More, the woman was notorious! Do you expect me to believe that?

MORE   Happily there are witnesses.

CROMWELL   You wrote a letter to her?

MORE   Yes, I wrote advising her to abstain from meddling with the affairs of Princes and the State. I have a copy of this letter—also witnessed.

CROMWELL   You have been cautious.

MORE   I like to keep my affairs regular.

CROMWELL   Sir Thomas, there is a more serious charge—

MORE   Charge?

CROMWELL   For want of a better word. In the May of 1526 the King published a book. (*He permits himself a little smile*) A theological work. It was called *A Defence of the Seven Sacraments.*

MORE   Yes. (*Bitterly*) For which he was named "Defender of the Faith," by His Holiness the Pope.

CROMWELL   By the Bishop of Rome. Or do you insist on "Pope"?

MORE   No, "Bishop of Rome" if you like. It doesn't alter his authority.

CROMWELL   Thank you, you come to the point very readily; what *is* that authority? As regards the Church in Europe; (*Approaching*) for example, the Church in England. What exactly *is* the Bishop of Rome's authority?

MORE   You will find it very ably set out and defended, Master Secretary, in the King's book.

CROMWELL   The book published under the King's name would be more accurate. You wrote that book.

MORE   I wrote no part of it.

CROMWELL   I do not mean you actually held the pen.

MORE   I merely answered to the best of my ability certain

questions on canon law which His Majesty put to me. As I was bound to do.

CROMWELL   Do you deny that you *instigated* it?

MORE   It was from first to last the King's own project. This is trivial, Master Cromwell.

CROMWELL   I should not think so if I were in your place.

MORE   Only two people know the truth of the matter. Myself and the King. And, whatever he may have said to you, he will not give evidence to support this accusation.

CROMWELL   Why not?

MORE   Because evidence is given on oath, and he will not perjure himself. If you don't know that, you don't yet know him.
(CROMWELL *looks at him viciously*)

CROMWELL (*Goes apart; formally*)   Sir Thomas More, is there anything you wish to say to me concerning the King's marriage with Queen Anne?

MORE (*Very still*)   I understood I was not to be asked that again.

CROMWELL   Evidently you understood wrongly. These charges—

MORE (*With a sudden, contemptuous sweep of his arm*)

117

They are terrors for children, Master Secretary—an empty cupboard! To frighten children in the dark, not me.

CROMWELL (*It is some time now since anybody treated him like this, and it costs him some effort to control his anger, but he does and even manages a little smile as one who sportingly admits defeat*) True . . . true, Sir Thomas, very apt. (*Then coldly*) To frighten a man, there must be something *in* the cupboard, must there not?

MORE (*Made wary again by the tone*) Yes, and there is nothing in it.

CROMWELL For the moment there is this: (*Picks up a paper and reads*) "I charge you with great ingratitude. I remind you of many benefits graciously given and ill received. I tell you that no King of England ever had nor could have so villainous a servant nor so traitorous a subject as yourself." (*During this,* MORE's *face goes ashen and his hand creeps up to his throat in an unconscious gesture of fear and protection.* CROMWELL *puts down the paper and says*) The words are not mine, Sir Thomas, but the King's. Believe that.

MORE I do. (*He lowers his hands, looks up again, and with just a spark of his old impudence*) I recognize the style. So I am brought here at last.

CROMWELL Brought? You brought yourself to where you stand now.

MORE Yes— Still, in another sense—I was brought.

118

CROMWELL Oh, yes. You may go home now. (*After a fractional hesitation,* MORE *goes, his face fearful and his step thoughtful, and he pauses uncertainly as* CROMWELL *calls after him*) For the present. (MORE *carries on, and exits*) I don't like him so well as I did. There's a man who raises the gale and won't come out of the harbor.

RICH (*A covert jeer*) Do you still think you can frighten him?

CROMWELL Oh, yes.

RICH (*Given pause*) What will you do?

CROMWELL We'll put something in the cupboard.

RICH (*Now definitely uneasy*) What?

CROMWELL (*As to an importunate child*) Whatever's necessary. The King's a man of conscience and he wants either Sir Thomas More to bless his marriage or Sir Thomas More destroyed.

RICH (*Shakily*) They seem odd alternatives, Secretary.

CROMWELL Do they? That's because you're not a man of conscience. If the King destroys a man, that's proof to the King that it must have been a bad man, the kind of man a man of conscience *ought* to destroy—and of course a bad man's blessing's not worth having. So either will do.

RICH (*Subdued*) I see.

CROMWELL Oh, there's no going back, Rich. I find we've made ourselves the keepers of this conscience. And it's ravenous. (*Exit* CROMWELL *and* RICH. *Enter* MORE. COMMON MAN *enters, removes a cloth, hears* MORE, *shakes head, exits*)

MORE (*Calling*) Boat! . . . Boat! . . . (*To himself*) Oh, come along, it's not as bad as that. . . . (*Calls*) Boat! (*Enter* NORFOLK. *He stops. Turning, pleased*) Howard! . . . I can't get home. They won't bring me a boat.

NORFOLK Do you blame them?

MORE Is it as bad as that?

NORFOLK It's every bit as bad as that!

MORE (*Gravely*) Then it's good of you to be seen with me.

NORFOLK (*Looking back, off*) I followed you.

MORE (*Surprised*) Were *you* followed?

NORFOLK Probably. (*Facing him*) So listen to what I have to say: You're behaving like a fool. You're behaving like a crank. You're not behaving like a gentleman— All right, that means nothing to you; but what about your friends?

MORE What about them?

NORFOLK Goddammit, you're dangerous to know!

MORE Then don't know me.

NORFOLK   There's something further . . . You must have realized by now there's a . . . policy, with regards to you. (MORE *nods*) The King is using me in it.

MORE   That's clever. That's Cromwell . . . You're between the upper and the nether millstones then.

NORFOLK   I am!

MORE   Howard, you must cease to know me.

NORFOLK   I do know you! I wish I didn't but I do!

MORE   I mean as a friend.

NORFOLK   You *are* my friend!

MORE   I can't relieve you of your obedience to the King, Howard. You must relieve yourself of our friendship. No one's safe now, and you have a son.

NORFOLK   You might as well advise a man to change the color of his hair! I'm fond of you, and there it is! You're fond of me, and there it is!

MORE   What's to be done then?

NORFOLK (*With deep appeal*)   Give in.

MORE (*Gently*)   I can't give in, Howard— (*A smile*) You might as well advise a man to change the color of his eyes. I can't. Our friendship's more mutable than *that*.

NORFOLK Oh, that's immutable, is it? The one fixed point in a world of changing friendships is that Thomas More will not give in!

MORE (*Urgent to explain*) To me it *has* to be, for that's myself! Affection goes as deep in me as you think, but only God is love right through, Howard; and *that's* my *self*.

NORFOLK And who are you? Goddammit, man, it's disproportionate! *We*'re supposed to be the arrogant ones, the proud, splenetic ones—and we've all given in! Why must you stand out? (*Quietly and quickly*) You'll break my heart.

MORE (*Moved*) We'll do it now, Howard: part, as friends, and meet as strangers.
(*He attempts to take* NORFOLK'S *hand*)

NORFOLK (*Throwing it off*) Daft, Thomas! Why d'you want to take your friendship from me? For friendship's sake! You say we'll meet as strangers and every word you've said confirms our friendship!

MORE (*Takes a last affectionate look at him*) Oh, that can be remedied. (*Walks away, turns; in a tone of deliberate insult*) Norfolk, you're a fool.

NORFOLK (*Starts; then smiles and folds his arms*) *You* can't place a quarrel; you haven't the style.

MORE Hear me out. You and your class have "given in"—as you rightly call it—because the religion of this country means nothing to you one way or the other.

NORFOLK Well, that's a foolish saying for a start; the nobility of England has always been—

MORE The nobility of England, my lord, would have snored through the Sermon on the Mount. But you'll labor like Thomas Aquinas over a rat-dog's pedigree. Now what's the name of those distorted creatures you're all breeding at the moment?

NORFOLK (*Steadily, but roused towards anger by* MORE's *tone*) An artificial quarrel's not a quarrel.

MORE Don't deceive yourself, my lord, we've had a quarrel since the day we met, our friendship was but sloth.

NORFOLK You can be cruel when you've a mind to be; but I've always known that.

MORE What's the name of those dogs? Marsh mastiffs? Bog beagles?

NORFOLK Water spaniels!

MORE And what would you do with a water spaniel that was afraid of water? You'd hang it! Well, as a spaniel is to water, so is a man to his own self. I will not give in because I oppose it—*I* do—not my pride, not my spleen, nor any other of my appetites but I do—I! (MORE *goes up to him and feels him up and down like an animal.* MARGARET's *voice is heard, well off, calling her father.* MORE's *attention is irresistibly caught by this; but he turns back determinedly to* NORFOLK) Is there no single sinew in the midst of this that serves no appetite of Norfolk's but is just Norfolk? There is! Give *that* some exercise, my lord!

MARGARET (*Off, nearer*) Father?

NORFOLK (*Breathing hard*) Thomas . . .

MORE Because as you stand, you'll go before your Maker in a very ill condition!
(*Enter* MARGARET, *below; she stops, amazed at them*)

NORFOLK Now steady, Thomas. . . .

MORE And he'll have to think that somewhere back along your pedigree—a bitch got over the wall!
(NORFOLK *lashes out at him; he ducks and winces. Exit* NORFOLK)

MARGARET Father! (*As he straightens up*) Father, what was that?

MORE That was Norfolk.
(*He looks after him wistfully.* ROPER *enters*)

ROPER (*Excited, almost gleeful*) Do you know, sir? Have you heard? (MORE *is still looking off, not answering. To* MARGARET) Have you told him?

MARGARET (*Gently*) We've been looking for you, Father.
(MORE *is still looking off*)

ROPER There's to be a new Act through Parliament, sir!

124

MORE (*Half-turning, half-attending*) Act?

ROPER Yes, sir—about the marriage!

MORE (*Indifferently*) Oh.
(*Turning back again.* ROPER *and* MARGARET *look at one another*)

MARGARET (*Puts a hand on his arm*) Father, by this Act, they're going to administer an oath.

MORE (*With instantaneous attention*) An oath! (*He looks from one to the other*) On what compulsion?

ROPER It's expected to be treason!

MORE (*Very still*) What is the oath?

ROPER (*Puzzled*) It's about the marriage, sir.

MORE But what is the wording?

ROPER We don't need to know the (*Contemptuously*) wording—we know what it will mean!

MORE It will mean what the words say! An oath is *made* of words! It may be possible to take it. Or avoid it. (*To* MARGARET) Have we a copy of the Bill?

MARGARET There's one coming out from the City.

MORE Then let's get home and look at it. Oh, I've no boat. (*He looks off again after* NORFOLK)

MARGARET (*Gently*)   Father, he tried to hit you.

MORE   Yes—I spoke, slightingly, of water spaniels. Let's get home.
(*He turns and sees* ROPER *excited and truculent*)

ROPER   But sir—

MORE   Now listen, Will. And, Meg, you listen, too, you know I know you well. God made the *angels* to show him splendor —as he made animals for innocence and plants for their simplicity. But Man he made to serve him wittily, in the tangle of his mind! If he suffers us to fall to such a case that there is no escaping, then we may stand to our tackle as best we can, and yes, Will, then we may clamor like champions . . . if we have the spittle for it. And no doubt it delights God to see splendor where He only looked for complexity. But it's God's part, not our own, to bring ourselves to that extremity! Our natural business lies in escaping— so let's get home and study this Bill.
(*Exit* MORE, ROPER *and* MARGARET. *Enter* COMMON MAN, *dragging a cage. The rear of the stage remains in moonlight. Now descends a rack, which remains suspended*)

COMMON MAN (*Aggrieved. Brings the basket on*)   Now look! . . . I don't suppose anyone enjoyed it any more than he did. Well, not much more. (*Takes from the basket and dons a coat and hat*) Jailer! (*Shrugs. Pushes basket off and arranges three chairs behind the table*) The pay scale being what it is they have to take a rather common type of man into the prison service. But it's a job. (*Admits* MORE *to jail, turns keys*) Bit nearer the knuckle than most perhaps, but it's a job like any other job— (*Sits on steps. Enter* CROMWELL, NORFOLK, CRANMER, *who sit, and* RICH, *who stands behind them.* MORE *enters the cage and lies down*) They'd let him out if they could, but for various reasons they can't. (*Twirling keys*) I'd let him out if I could but I can't. Not without taking up residence in there myself. And he's in there already, so what'd be the point? You know the old adage? "Better a live rat than a dead lion," and that's about it. (*An envelope descends swiftly before him. He opens it and reads*) "With reference to the old adage: Thomas Cromwell was found guilty of High Treason and executed on 28 July, 1540. Norfolk was found guilty of High Treason and should have been executed on 27 January, 1547, but on the night of 26 January, the King died of syphilis and wasn't able to sign the warrant. Thomas Cranmer"—Archbishop of Canterbury, (*Jerking thumb*) that's the other one—"was burned alive on 21 March, 1556." (*He is about to conclude but sees a postscript*) Oh. "Richard Rich became a Knight and Solicitor-General, a Baron and Lord Chancellor, and died in his bed." So did I. And so, I hope, will all of you. (*He goes to* MORE *and rouses him*) Wake up, Sir Thomas.

MORE (*Rousing*) What, again?

JAILER Sorry, sir.

MORE (*Flops back*) What time is it?

JAILER One o'clock, sir.

MORE Oh, this is iniquitous!

JAILER (*Anxiously*) Sir.

MORE (*Sitting up*) All right. (*Putting on slippers*) Who's there?

JAILER The Secretary, the Duke, and the Archbishop.

MORE I'm flattered. (*He stands, claps hand to hip*) Ooh! (*Preceded by* JAILER *he limps across the stage; he has aged and is pale, but his manner, though wary, is relaxed; while that of the Commission is bored, tense, and jumpy*)

NORFOLK (*Looks at him*) A seat for the prisoner. (*While* JAILER *brings a stool from under the stairs and* MORE *sits on it,* NORFOLK *rattles off*) This is the Seventh Commission to inquire into the case of Sir Thomas More, appointed by His Majesty's Council. Have you anything to say?

MORE No. (*To* JAILER) Thank you.

NORFOLK (*Sitting back*) Master Secretary.

CROMWELL Sir Thomas— (*He breaks off*) Do the witnesses attend?

RICH Secretary.

JAILER Sir.

CROMWELL (*To* JAILER) Nearer! (*He advances a bit*) Come where you can hear! (JAILER *takes up stance by* RICH. *To* MORE) Sir Thomas, you have seen this document before?

MORE   Many times.

CROMWELL   It is the Act of Succession. These are the names
of those who have sworn to it.

MORE   I have, as you say, seen it before.

CROMWELL   Will you swear to it?

MORE   No.

NORFOLK   Thomas, we must know plainly—

CROMWELL *(Throws down document)*   Your Grace, *please!*

NORFOLK   Master Cromwell!
(They regard one another in hatred)

CROMWELL   I beg Your Grace's pardon.
(Sighing, rests his head in his hands)

NORFOLK   Thomas, we must know plainly whether you recognize the offspring of Queen Anne as heirs to His Majesty.

MORE   The King in Parliament tells me that they are. Of
course I recognize them.

NORFOLK   Will you swear that you do?

MORE   Yes.

NORFOLK   Then why won't you swear to the Act?

CROMWELL (*Impatiently*) Because there is more than that *in* the Act.

NORFOLK Is that it?

MORE (*After a pause*) Yes.

NORFOLK Then we must find out what it is in the Act that he objects to!

CROMWELL Brilliant. (NORFOLK *rounds on him*) God's wounds!

CRANMER (*Hastily*) Your Grace— May I try?

NORFOLK Certainly. I've no pretension to be an expert in police work.
(*During the next speech* CROMWELL *straightens up and folds arms resignedly*)

CRANMER (*Clears his throat fussily*) Sir Thomas, it states in the preamble that the King's former marriage, to the Lady Catherine, was unlawful, she being previously his brother's wife and the—er—"Pope" having no authority to sanction it. (*Gently*) Is that what you deny? (*No reply*) Is that what you dispute? (*No reply*) Is that what you are not sure of? (*No reply*)

NORFOLK Thomas, you insult the King and His Council in the person of the Lord Archbishop!

MORE I insult no one. I will not take the oath. I will not tell you why I will not.

130

NORFOLK Then your reasons must be treasonable!

MORE Not "must be"; may be.

NORFOLK It's a fair assumption!

MORE The law requires more than an assumption; the law requires a fact.
(CROMWELL *looks at him and away again*)

CRANMER I cannot judge your legal standing in the case; but until I know the *ground* of your objections, I can only guess your spiritual standing too.

MORE (*For a second furiously affronted; then humor overtakes him*) If you're willing to guess at that, Your Grace, it should be a small matter to guess my objections.

CROMWELL (*Quickly*) You do have objections to the Act?

NORFOLK (*Happily*) Well, we know *that*, Cromwell!

MORE You don't, my lord. You may *suppose* I have objections. All you *know* is that I will not swear to it. From sheer delight to give you trouble it might be.

NORFOLK Is it material why you won't?

MORE It's most material. For refusing to swear, my goods are forfeit and I am condemned to life imprisonment. You cannot lawfully harm me further. But if you were right in supposing I had reasons for refusing and right again in supposing my reasons to be treasonable, the law would let you cut my head off.

NORFOLK (*He has followed with some difficulty*) Oh yes.

CROMWELL (*An admiring murmur*) Oh, well done, Sir Thomas. I've been trying to make that clear to His Grace for some time.

NORFOLK (*Hardly responds to the insult; his face is gloomy and disgusted*) Oh, confound all this . . . (*With real dignity*) I'm not a scholar, as Master Cromwell never tires of pointing out, and frankly I don't know whether the marriage was lawful or not. But damn it, Thomas, look at those names . . . You know those men! Can't you do what I did, and come with us, for fellowship?

MORE (*Moved*) And when we stand before God, and you are sent to Paradise for doing according to your conscience, and I am damned for not doing according to mine, will you come with me, for fellowship?

CRANMER So those of us whose names are there are damned, Sir Thomas?

MORE I don't know, Your Grace. I have no window to look into another man's conscience. I condemn no one.

CRANMER Then the matter is capable of question?

MORE Certainly.

CRANMER   But that you owe obedience to your King is not capable of question. So weigh a doubt against a certainty— and sign.

MORE   Some men think the Earth is round, others think it flat; it is a matter capable of question. But if it is flat, will the King's command make it round? And if it is round, will the King's command flatten it? No, I will not sign.

CROMWELL (*Leaping up, with ceremonial indignation*)   Then you have more regard to your own doubt than you have to his command!

MORE   For myself, I have no doubt.

CROMWELL   No doubt of what?

MORE   No doubt of my grounds for refusing this oath. Grounds I will tell to the King alone, and which you, Master Secretary, will not trick out of me.

NORFOLK   Thomas—

MORE   Oh, gentlemen, can't I go to bed?

CROMWELL   You don't seem to appreciate the seriousness of your position.

MORE   I defy anyone to live in that cell for a year and not appreciate the seriousness of his position.

CROMWELL   Yet the State has harsher punishments.

MORE You threaten like a dockside bully.

CROMWELL How should I threaten?

MORE Like a Minister of State, with justice!

CROMWELL Oh, justice is what you're threatened with.

MORE Then I'm not threatened.

NORFOLK Master Secretary, I think the prisoner may retire as he requests. Unless you, my lord—

CRANMER (*Pettishly*) No, I see no purpose in prolonging the interview.

NORFOLK Then good night, Thomas.

MORE (*Hesitates*) Might I have one or two more books?

CROMWELL You have books?

MORE Yes.

CROMWELL I didn't know; you shouldn't have.

MORE (*Turns to go, pauses. Desperately*) May I see my family?

CROMWELL No! (MORE *returns to cell*) Jailer!

JAILER Sir!

CROMWELL   Have you ever heard the prisoner speak of the King's divorce, or the King's Supremacy of the Church, or the King's marriage?

JAILER   No, sir, not a word.

CROMWELL   If he does, you will of course report it to the Lieutenant.

JAILER   Of course, sir.

CROMWELL   You will swear an oath to that effect.

JAILER (*Cheerfully*)   Certainly, sir!

CROMWELL   Archbishop?

CRANMER (*Laying the cross of his vestment on the table*) Place your left hand on this and raise your right hand— take your hat off— Now say after me: I swear by my immortal soul— (JAILER, *overlapping, repeats the oath with him*) —that I will report truly anything said by Sir Thomas More against the King, the Council or the State of the Realm. So help me God. Amen.

JAILER (*Overlapping*)   So help me God. Amen.

CROMWELL   And there's fifty guineas in it if you do.

JAILER (*Looks at him gravely*)   Yes, sir.
(*He goes*)

CRANMER (*Hastily*)   That's not to tempt you into perjury, my man!

JAILER   No, sir! (*At exit he pauses; to audience*) Fifty guineas isn't tempting; fifty guineas is alarming. If he'd left it at swearing . . . But fifty— That's serious money. If it's worth that much now it's worth my neck presently. (*With decision*) I want no part of it. They can sort it out between them. I feel my deafness coming on.
(*Exit* JAILER. *The Commission rises*)

CROMWELL   Rich!

RICH   Secretary?

CROMWELL   Tomorrow morning, remove the prisoner's books.

NORFOLK   Is that necessary?

CROMWELL (*Suppressed exasperation*)   Norfolk. With regards this case, the King is becoming impatient.

NORFOLK   Aye, with you.

CROMWELL   With all of us. (*He walks over to the rack*) You know the King's impatience, how commodious it is!
(NORFOLK *and* CRANMER *exit.* CROMWELL *is brooding over the instrument of torture*)

RICH   Secretary!

CROMWELL (*Abstracted*)   Yes . . .

RICH   Sir Redvers Llewellyn has retired.

CROMWELL (*Not listening*) Mm . . .

RICH (*Goes to the other end of the rack and faces him. With some indignation*) The Attorney-General for Wales. His post is vacant. You said I might approach you.

CROMWELL (*Contemptuous impatience*) Oh, not *now* . . . (*Broods*) He must submit, the alternatives are bad. While More's alive the King's conscience breaks into fresh stinking flowers every time he gets from bed. And if I bring about More's death—I plant my own, I think. There's no other good solution! He must submit! (*He whirls the windlass of the rack, producing a startling clatter from the ratchet. They look at each other. He turns it again slowly, shakes his head and lets go*) No; the King will not permit it. (*He walks away*) We have to find some gentler way.
(*The scene change commences as he says this, and exit* RICH *and* CROMWELL. *From night it becomes morning, cold gray light from off the gray water. Enter* JAILER *and* MARGARET)

JAILER Wake up, Sir Thomas! Your family's here!

MORE (*Starting up. A great cry*) Margaret! What's this? You can visit me? (*Thrusts his arms through the cage*) Meg. Meg. (*She goes to him. Then horrified*) For God's sake, Meg, they've not put *you* in here?

JAILER (*Reassuringly*) No-o-o, sir. Just a visit; a short one.

MORE (*Excited*) Jailer, jailer, let me out of this.

JAILER Yes, sir. I'm allowed to let you out.

MORE Thank you. (*Goes to the door of the cage, gabbling while* JAILER *unlocks it*) Thank you, thank you.
(*He comes out. He and she regard each other; then she drops into a curtsy*)

MARGARET Good morning, Father.

MORE (*Ecstatic, wraps her to him*) Oh, good morning— Good morning. (*Enter* ALICE, *supported by* ROPER. *She, like* MORE, *has aged and is poorly dressed*) Good morning, Alice. Good morning, Will.
(ROPER *is staring at the rack in horror.* ALICE *approaches* MORE *and peers at him technically*)

ALICE (*Almost accusatory*) Husband, how do you do?

MORE (*Smiling over* MARGARET) As well as need be, Alice. Very happy now. Will?

ROPER This is an awful place!

MORE Except it's keeping me from you, my dears, it's not so bad. Remarkably like any other place.

ALICE (*Looks up critically*) It drips!

MORE Yes. Too near the river.
(ALICE *goes apart and sits, her face bitter*)

MARGARET (*Disengages from him, takes basket from her mother*) We've brought you some things. (*Shows him. There is constraint between them*) Some cheese . . .

MORE Cheese.

MARGARET And a custard . . .

MORE A custard!

MARGARET And, these other things . . .
(*She doesn't look at him*)

ROPER And a bottle of wine.
(*Offering it*)

MORE Oh. (*Mischievously*) Is it good, son Roper?

ROPER I don't know, sir.

MORE (*Looks at them, puzzled*) Well.

ROPER Sir, come out! Swear to the Act! Take the oath and
come out!

MORE Is this why they let you come?

ROPER Yes . . . Meg's under oath to persuade you.

MORE (*Coldly*) That was silly, Meg. How did you come to
do that?

MARGARET I wanted to!

MORE You want me to swear to the Act of Succession?

MARGARET "God more regards the thoughts of the heart than the words of the mouth." Or so you've always told me.

MORE Yes.

MARGARET Then say the words of the oath and in your heart think otherwise.

MORE What is an oath then but words we say to God?

MARGARET That's very neat.

MORE Do you mean it isn't true?

MARGARET No, it's true.

MORE Then it's a poor argument to call it "neat," Meg. When a man takes an oath, Meg, he's holding his own self in his own hands. Like water. (*He cups his hands*) And if he opens his fingers *then*—he needn't hope to find himself again. Some men aren't capable of this, but I'd be loathe to think your father one of them.

MARGARET In any State that was half good, you would be raised up high, not here, for what you've done already. It's not your fault the State's three-quarters bad. Then if you elect to suffer for it, you elect yourself a hero.

MORE That's very neat. But look now . . . If we lived in a State where virtue was profitable, common sense would make us good, and greed would make us saintly. And we'd live like animals or angels in the happy land that *needs* no heroes.

But since in fact we see that avarice, anger, envy, pride, sloth, lust and stupidity commonly profit far beyond humility, chastity, fortitude, justice and thought, and have to choose, to be human at all . . . why then perhaps we *must* stand fast a little—even at the risk of being heroes.

MARGARET (*Emotionally*) But in reason! Haven't you done as much as God can reasonably *want*?

MORE Well . . . finally . . . it isn't a matter of reason; finally it's a matter of love.

ALICE (*Hostile*) You're content, then, to be shut up here with mice and rats when you might be home with us!

MORE (*Flinching*) Content? If they'd open a crack that wide (*Between finger and thumb*) I'd be through it. (*To* MARGARET) Well, has Eve run out of apples?

MARGARET I've not yet told you what the house is like, without you.

MORE Don't, Meg.

MARGARET What we do in the evenings, now that you're not there.

MORE Meg, have done!

MARGARET We sit in the dark because we've no candles. And we've no talk because we're wondering what they're doing to you here.

MORE The King's more merciful than you. He doesn't use the rack.
(*Enter* JAILER)

JAILER Two minutes to go, sir. I thought you'd like to know.

MORE Two minutes!

JAILER Till seven o'clock, sir. Sorry. Two minutes.
(*Exit* JAILER)

MORE Jailer! (*Seizes* ROPER *by the arm*) Will—go to him, talk to him, keep him occupied—
(*Propelling him after* JAILER)

ROPER How, sir?

MORE Anyhow! Have you got any money?

ROPER (*Eagerly*) Yes!

MORE No, don't try and bribe him! Let him play for it; he's got a pair of dice. And talk to him, you understand! And take this— (*He hands him the wine*) and mind you share it —do it properly, Will! (ROPER *nods vigorously and exits*) Now listen, you must leave the country. All of you must leave the country.

MARGARET And leave you here?

MORE It makes no difference, Meg; they won't let you see me again. (*Breathlessly, a prepared speech under pressure*) You must all go on the same day, but not on the same boat; different boats from different ports—

MARGARET   After the trial, then.

MORE   There'll be no trial, they have no case. Do this for me, I beseech you?

MARGARET   Yes.

MORE   Alice? (*She turns her back*) Alice, I command you!

ALICE (*Harshly*)   Right!

MORE (*Looks into the basket*)   Oh, this is splendid; I know who packed this.

ALICE (*Harshly*)   I packed it.

MORE   Yes. (*He eats a morsel*) You still make superlative custard, Alice.

ALICE   Do I?

MORE   That's a nice dress you have on.

ALICE   It's my cooking dress.

MORE   It's very nice anyway. Nice color.

ALICE (*Turns. Quietly*)   By God, you think very little of me. (*Mounting bitterness*) I know I'm a fool. But I'm no such

143

fool as at this time to be lamenting for my dresses! Or to relish complimenting on my custard!

MORE (*Regarding her with frozen attention. He nods once or twice*) I am well rebuked. (*He holds out his hands*) Al—

ALICE No!
(*She remains where she is, glaring at him*)

MORE (*He is in great fear of her*) I am faint when I think of the worst that they may do to me. But worse than that would be to go with you not understanding why I go.

ALICE I don't!

MORE (*Just hanging on to his self-possession*) Alice, if you can tell me that you understand, I think I can make a good death, if I have to.

ALICE Your death's no "good" to me!

MORE Alice, you must tell me that you understand!

ALICE I don't! (*She throws it straight at his head*) I don't believe this had to happen.

MORE (*His face is drawn*) If you say that, Alice, I don't see how I'm to face it.

ALICE It's the truth!

MORE (*Gasping*) You're an honest woman.

ALICE   Much good may it do me! I'll tell you what I'm afraid of: that when you've gone, I shall hate you for it.

MORE (*Turns from her, his face working*)   Well, you mustn't, Alice, that's all. (*Swiftly she crosses the stage to him; he turns and they clasp each other fiercely*) You mustn't, you—

ALICE (*Covers his mouth with her hand*)   S-s-sh . . . As for understanding, I understand you're the best man that I ever met or am likely to; and if you go—well, God knows why I suppose—though as God's my witness God's kept deadly quiet about it! And if anyone wants my opinion of the King and his Council they've only to ask for it!

MORE   Why, it's a lion I married! A lion! A lion! (*He breaks away from her, his face shining*) Say what you may—this custard's very good. It's very, very good.
(*He puts his face in his hands;* ALICE *and* MARGARET *comfort him;* ROPER *and* JAILER *erupt onto the stage above, wrangling fiercely*)

JAILER   It's no good, sir! I know what you're up to! And it can't be done!

ROPER   Another minute, man!

JAILER (*Descending; to* MORE)   Sorry, sir, time's up!

ROPER (*Gripping his shoulder from behind*)   For pity's sake!

JAILER (*Shaking him off*)   Now don't do that, sir! Sir Thomas, the ladies will have to go now!

MORE   You said seven o'clock!

JAILER   It's seven now. You must understand my position, sir.

MORE   But one more minute!

MARGARET   Only a little while—give us a little while!

JAILER (*Reprovingly*)   Now, miss, you don't want to get me into trouble.

ALICE   Do as you're told. Be off at once!
(*The first stroke of seven is heard on a heavy, deliberate bell, which continues, reducing what follows to a babble*)

JAILER (*Taking* MARGARET *firmly by the upper arm*)   Now come along, miss; you'll get your father into trouble as well as me. (ROPER *descends and grabs him*) Are you obstructing me, sir? (MARGARET *embraces* MORE *and dashes up the stairs and exits, followed by* ROPER. *Taking* ALICE *gingerly by the arm*) Now, my lady, no trouble!

ALICE (*Throwing him off as she rises*)   Don't put your muddy hand on me!

JAILER   Am I to call the guard then? Then come on!
(ALICE, *facing him, puts foot on bottom stair and so retreats before him, backwards*)

MORE   For God's sake, man, we're saying goodbye!

JAILER   You don't know what you're asking, sir. You don't know how you're watched.

ALICE   Filthy, stinking, gutter-bred turnkey!

JAILER   Call me what you like, ma'am; you've got to go.

ALICE   I'll see you suffer for this!

JAILER   You're doing your husband no good!

MORE   Alice, goodbye, my love!
(*On this, the last stroke of the seven sounds.* ALICE *raises her hand, turns, and with considerable dignity, exits.* JAILER *stops at the head of the stairs and addresses* MORE, *who, still crouching, turns from him, facing audience*)

JAILER (*Reasonably*)   You understand my position, sir, there's nothing I can do; I'm a plain, simple man and just want to keep out of trouble.

MORE (*Cries out passionately*)   Oh, Sweet Jesus! These plain, simple men!
(*Immediately music, portentous and heraldic, is heard. Bars, rack and cage are flown swiftly upwards. The lighting changes from cold gray to warm yellow, re-creating a warm interior. Small coat of arms comes down and hangs, followed by large coat of arms above stairs, then two medium coats of arms. Then the largest coat of arms appears. During this the* JAILER *takes off jailer's coat, throws it off, takes off the small chair and moves armchair to the center. Moves the table under the stairs. He brings on the jury bench, takes hats*)

from the basket and puts them on poles with a juryman's hat, takes jailer's hat off head and puts it on a pole. Seven are plain gray hats, four are those worn by the STEWARD, BOATMAN, INNKEEPER *and* JAILER. *And the last is another of the plain gray ones. He takes a portfolio from the basket and puts it on the table, and pushes basket into a corner. He then brings on two throne chairs. While he is still doing this, and just before coats of arms have finished their descent, enter* CROMWELL. *He ringingly addresses the audience as soon as the music ends)*

CROMWELL *(Indicating descending props)*
>   What Englishman can behold without Awe
>   The Canvas and the Rigging of the Law!

(Brief fanfare)
>   Forbidden here the galley-master's whip—
>   Hearts of Oak, in the Law's Great Ship!

(Brief fanfare. To COMMON MAN *who is tiptoeing discreetly off-stage)* Where are you going?

COMMON MAN   I've finished here, sir.

CROMWELL   You're the Foreman of the Jury.

COMMON MAN   Oh no, sir.

CROMWELL   You are John Dauncey. A general dealer?

COMMON MAN *(Gloomily)*   Yes, sir?

CROMWELL *(Resuming his rhetorical stance)*   Foreman of the Jury. Does the cap fit?

COMMON MAN (*Puts on the gray hat. It fits*)   Yes, sir.

CROMWELL
>So, now we'll apply the good, plain sailor's art,
>And fix these quicksands on the Law's plain chart!
(*Several narrow panels, orange and bearing the monogram
"HR VIII" in gold letters, are lowered. Renewed, more pro-
longed fanfare; during which enter* CRANMER *and* NORFOLK,
who sit on throne chairs. On their entry MORE *and* FOREMAN
rise. As soon as the fanfare is finished NORFOLK *speaks*)

NORFOLK (*Takes refuge behind a rigorously official manner*)
Sir Thomas More, you are called before us here at the Hall
of Westminster to answer charge of High Treason. Nevertheless, and though you have heinously offended the King's
Majesty, we hope if you will even now forthink and repent
of your obstinate opinions, you may still taste his gracious
pardon.

MORE   My lords, I thank you. Howbeit I make my petition
to Almighty God that He will keep me in this, my honest
mind, to the last hour that I shall live . . . As for the matters
you may charge me with, I fear, from my present weakness,
that neither my wit nor my memory will serve to make
sufficient answers . . . I should be glad to sit down.

NORFOLK   Be seated. Master Secretary Cromwell, have you the
charge?

CROMWELL   I have, my lord.

NORFOLK   Then read the charge.

CROMWELL (*Formally*) That you did conspire traitorously and maliciously to deny and deprive our liege lord Henry of his undoubted certain title, Supreme Head of the Church in England.

MORE (*With surprise, shock, and indignation*) But I have never denied this title!

CROMWELL You refused the oath tendered to you at the Tower and elsewhere—

MORE (*Again shocked and indignant*) Silence is not denial. And for my silence I am punished, with imprisonment. Why have I been called again?
(*At this point he is sensing that the trial has been in some way rigged*)

NORFOLK On a charge of High Treason, Sir Thomas.

CROMWELL For which the punishment is *not* imprisonment.

MORE Death . . . comes for us all, my lords. Yes, even for Kings he comes, to whom amidst all their Royalty and brute strength he will neither kneel nor make them any reverence nor pleasantly desire them to come forth, but roughly grasp them by the very breast and rattle them until they be stark dead! So causing their bodies to be buried in a pit and sending *them* to a judgment . . . whereof at their death their success is uncertain.

CROMWELL Treason enough here!

NORFOLK   The death of Kings is not in question, Sir Thomas.

MORE   Nor mine, I trust, until I'm proven guilty.

NORFOLK (*Leaning forward urgently*)   Your life lies in your own hand, Thomas, as it always has.

MORE (*Absorbs this*)   For our own deaths, my lord, yours and mine, dare we for shame enter the Kingdom with ease, when Our Lord Himself entered with so much pain?
(*And now he faces* CROMWELL, *his eyes sparkling with suspicion*)

CROMWELL   Now, Sir Thomas, you stand upon your silence.

MORE   I do.

CROMWELL   But, Gentlemen of the Jury, there are many kinds of silence. Consider first the silence of a man when he is dead. Let us say we go into the room where he is lying; and let us say it is in the dead of night—there's nothing like darkness for sharpening the ear; and we listen. What do we hear? Silence. What does it betoken, this silence? Nothing. This is silence, pure and simple. But consider another case. Suppose I were to draw a dagger from my sleeve and make to kill the prisoner with it, and suppose their lordships there, instead of crying out for me to stop or crying out for help to stop me, maintained their silence. That *would* betoken! It would betoken a willingness that I should do it, and under the law they would be guilty with me. So silence can, according to circumstances, speak. Consider, now, the circumstances of the prisoner's silence. The oath was put to good and faithful subjects up and down the country and they had declared His Grace's title to be just and good. And when it came to the prisoner he refused. He calls this silence. Yet is there a man in this court, is there a man in this country, who does not *know* Sir Thomas More's opinion of the King's title? Of course not! But how can that be? Because this silence betokened—nay, this silence *was* not silence at all but most eloquent denial.

MORE (*With some of the academic's impatience for a shoddy line of reasoning*) Not so, Master Secretary, the maxim is "qui tacet consentire." (*Turns to* COMMON MAN) The maxim of the law is (*Very carefully*) "Silence gives consent." If, therefore, you wish to construe what my silence "betokened," you must construe that I consented, not that I denied.

CROMWELL Is that what the world in fact construes from it? Do you pretend that is what you *wish* the world to construe from it?

MORE The world must construe according to its wits. This Court must construe according to the law.

CROMWELL I put it to the Court that the prisoner is perverting the law—making smoky what should be a clear light to discover to the Court his own wrongdoing!
(CROMWELL's *official indignation is slipping into genuine anger and* MORE *responds*)

MORE The law is not a "light" for you or any man to see by; the law is not an instrument of any kind. (*To the* FORE-

MAN) The law is a causeway upon which, so long as he keeps to it, a citizen may walk safely. (*Earnestly addressing him*) In matters of conscience—

CROMWELL (*Smiling bitterly*) The conscience, the conscience . . .

MORE (*Turning*) The word is not familiar to you?

CROMWELL By God, too familiar! I am very used to hear it in the mouths of criminals!

MORE I am used to hear bad men misuse the name of God, yet God exists. (*Turning back*) In matters of conscience, the loyal subject is more bounden to be loyal *to* his conscience than to any other thing.

CROMWELL (*Breathing hard; straight at* MORE) And so provide a noble motive for his frivolous self-conceit!

MORE (*Earnestly*) It is not so, Master Cromwell—very and pure necessity for respect of my own soul.

CROMWELL Your own self, you mean!

MORE Yes, a man's soul is his self!

CROMWELL (*Thrusts his face into* MORE's. *They hate each other and each other's standpoint*) A miserable thing, whatever you call it, that lives like a bat in a Sunday School! A shrill incessant pedagogue about its own salvation—but nothing to say of your place in the State! Under the King! In a great native country!

MORE (*Not untouched*) Is it my place to say "good" to the State's sickness? Can I help my King by giving him lies when he asks for truth? Will you help England by populating her with liars?

CROMWELL (*Backs away. His face stiff with malevolence*) My lords, I wish to call (*He raises his voice*) Sir Richard Rich! (*Enter* RICH. *He is now splendidly official, in dress and bearing; even* NORFOLK *is a bit impressed*) Sir Richard. (*Indicating* CRANMER)

CRANMER (*Proffering Bible*) I do solemnly swear . . .

RICH I do solemnly swear that the evidence I shall give before the Court shall be the truth, the whole truth, and nothing but the truth.

CRANMER (*Discreetly*) So help me God, Sir Richard.

RICH So help me God.

NORFOLK Take your stand there, Sir Richard.

CROMWELL Now, Rich, on 12 March, you were at the Tower?

RICH I was.

CROMWELL With what purpose?

RICH I was sent to carry away the prisoner's books.

CROMWELL   Did you talk with the prisoner?

RICH   Yes.

CROMWELL   Did you talk about the King's Supremacy of the Church?

RICH   Yes.

CROMWELL   What did you say?

RICH   I said to him: "Supposing there was an Act of Parliament to say that I, Richard Rich, were to be King, would not you, Master More, take me for King?" "That I would," he said, "for then you would be King."

CROMWELL   Yes?

RICHARD   Then he said—

NORFOLK (*Sharply*)   The prisoner?

RICH   Yes, my lord. "But I will put you a higher case," he said. "How if there were an Act of Parliament to say that God should not be God?"

MORE   This is true; and then you said—

NORFOLK   Silence! Continue.

RICH   I said, "Ah, but I will put you a middle case. Parliament has made our King Head of the Church. Why will you not accept him?"

NORFOLK (*Strung up*) Well?

RICH   Then he said Parliament had no power to do it.

NORFOLK   Repeat the prisoner's words!

RICH   He said, "Parliament has not the competence." Or words to that effect.

CROMWELL   He denied the title?

RICH   He did.
(*All look to* MORE, *but he looks to* RICH)

MORE   In good faith, Rich, I am sorrier for your perjury than my peril.

NORFOLK   Do you deny this?

MORE   Yes! My lords, if I were a man who heeded not the taking of an oath, you know well I need not to be here. Now I will take an oath! If what Master Rich has said is true, then I pray I may never see God in the face! Which I would not say were it otherwise for anything on earth.

CROMWELL (*To* FOREMAN, *calmly, technically*) That is not evidence.

MORE   Is it probable—is it probable—that after so long a silence on this, the very point so urgently sought of me, I should open my mind to such a man as that?

CROMWELL (*To* RICH) Do you wish to modify your testimony?

RICH No, Secretary.

MORE There were two other men! Southwell and Palmer!

CROMWELL Unhappily, Sir Richard Southwell and Master Palmer are both in Ireland on the King's business. (MORE *gestures helplessly*) It has no bearing. I have their deposition here in which the Court will see they state that being busy with the prisoner's books they did not hear what was said.
(*Hands deposition to* FOREMAN, *who examines it with much seriousness*)

MORE If I had really said this is it not obvious he would instantly have called these men to witness?

CROMWELL Sir Richard, have you anything to add?

RICH Nothing, Mr. Secretary.

NORFOLK Sir Thomas?

MORE (*Looking at* FOREMAN) To what purpose? I am a dead man. (*To* CROMWELL) You have your desire of me. What you have hunted me for is not my actions, but the thoughts of my heart. It is a long road you have opened. For first men will disclaim their hearts and presently they will have no hearts. God help the people whose Statesmen walk your road.

NORFOLK Then the witness may withdraw.
(RICH *crosses the stage, watched by* MORE)

MORE I *have* one question to ask the witness. (RICH *stops*)
That's a chain of office you are wearing. (*Reluctantly* RICH
faces him) May I see it? (NORFOLK *motions him to approach.* MORE *examines the medallion*) The red dragon.
(*To* CROMWELL) What's this?

CROMWELL Sir Richard is appointed Attorney-General for
Wales.

MORE (*Looking into* RICH'S *face, with pain and amusement*)
For Wales? Why, Richard, it profits a man nothing to give
his soul for the whole world . . . But for Wales!
(*Exit* RICH, *stiff-faced, but infrangibly dignified*)

CROMWELL Now I must ask the Court's indulgence! I have a
message for the prisoner from the King. (*Urgently*) Sir
Thomas, I am empowered to tell you that even now—

MORE No no, it cannot be.

CROMWELL The case rests! (NORFOLK *is staring at* MORE)
My lord!

NORFOLK The jury will retire and consider the evidence.

CROMWELL Considering the evidence it shouldn't be necessary for them to retire. (*Standing over* FOREMAN) Is it necessary?

FOREMAN (*Shakes his head*) No, sir!

NORFOLK Then is the prisoner guilty or not guilty?

FOREMAN Guilty, my lord!

NORFOLK (*Leaping to his feet; all rise save* MORE) Prisoner at the bar, you have been found guilty of High Treason. The sentence of the Court—

MORE My lord! (NORFOLK *breaks off.* MORE *has a sly smile. From this point to end of play his manner is of one who has fulfilled all his obligations and will now consult no interests but his own*) My lord, when I was practicing the law, the manner was to ask the prisoner *before* pronouncing sentence, if he had anything to say.

NORFOLK (*Flummoxed*) Have you anything to say?

MORE Yes. (*He rises; all others sit*) To avoid this I have taken every path my winding wits would find. Now that the Court has determined to condemn me, God knoweth how, I will discharge my mind . . . concerning my indictment and the King's title. The indictment is grounded in an Act of Parliament which is directly repugnant to the Law of God. The King in Parliament cannot bestow the Supremacy of the Church because it is a Spiritual Supremacy! And more to this the immunity of the Church is promised both in Magna Carta and the King's own Coronation Oath!

CROMWELL Now we plainly see that you *are* malicious!

MORE Not so, Master Secretary! (*He pauses, and launches, very quietly, ruminatively, into his final stock-taking*) I am the King's true subject, and pray for him and all the realm . . . I do none harm, I say none harm, I think none harm. And if this be not enough to keep a man alive, in good faith I long not to live . . . I have, since I came into prison, been several times in such a case that I thought to die within the hour, and I thank Our Lord I was never sorry for it, but rather sorry when it passed. And therefore, my poor body is at the King's pleasure. Would God my death might do him some good . . . (*With a great flash of scorn and anger*) Nevertheless, it is not for the Supremacy that you have sought my blood—but because I would not bend to the marriage!

(*Immediately the scene change commences, while* NORFOLK *reads the sentence*)

NORFOLK Prisoner at the bar, you have been found guilty on the charge of High Treason. The sentence of the Court is that you shall be taken from this Court to the Tower, thence to the place of execution, and there your head shall be stricken from your body, and may God have mercy on your soul!

(*The trappings of justice are flown upwards.* NORFOLK *and* CRANMER *exit with chairs. The lights are dimmed save for three areas: spots, left, center, and right front, and a black arch cutout is lowered. Through this arch—where the ax and the block are silhouetted against a light of steadily increasing brilliance—comes the murmur of a large crowd, formalized almost into a chant. The* FOREMAN *doffs cap, and as* COMMON MAN *he removes the prisoner's chair and the two benches.* CROMWELL *pushes the table off, takes a small black mask from basket and puts it on* COMMON MAN. *The* COMMON MAN *thus becomes the traditional Headsman. He ascends the stairs, sets up the block from its trap, gets the ax and then straddles his legs. At once the crowd falls silent. Exit* CROMWELL, *dragging basket.* NORFOLK *joins* MORE *in the center spot.* CRANMER *takes his position on the rostrum. The* WOMAN *goes under the stairs)* I can come no further, Thomas. *(Proffering a goblet)* Here, drink this.

MORE   My Master had easel and gall, not wine, given him to drink. Let me be going.

MARGARET   Father! *(She runs to him in the center spot and flings herself upon him)* Father! Father, Father, Father, Father!

MORE   Have patience, Margaret, and trouble not thyself. Death comes for us all; even at our birth— *(He holds her head and looks down at it for a moment in recollection)* — even at our birth, death does but stand aside a little. And every day he looks towards us and muses somewhat to himself whether that day or the next he will draw nigh. It is the law of nature, and the will of God. *(He disengages from her. Dispassionately)* You have long known the secrets of my heart.

*(*MARGARET *exits with* NORFOLK*)*

WOMAN   Sir Thomas! *(He stops)* Remember me, Sir Thomas? When you were Chancellor, you gave a false judgment against me. Remember that now.

MORE Woman, you see how I am occupied. (*With sudden decision goes to her in the left spot. Crisply*) I remember your matter well, and if I had to give sentence now I assure you I should not alter it. You have no injury; so go your way; and content yourself; and trouble me not! (*She exits. He walks swiftly to the stairs, then stops, realizing that* CRANMER, *carrying his Bible, has followed him. Quite kindly*) I beseech Your Grace, go back. (*Offended,* CRANMER *does so. The lighting is now complete, i.e., darkness save for three areas of light, the one at cutout arch now dazzlingly brilliant. When* MORE *gets to head of stairs by the Headsman, he turns to Headsman*) Friend, be not afraid of your office. You send me to God.

CRANMER (*Envious rather than waspish*) You're very sure of that, Sir Thomas.
(*He exits*)

MORE (*Takes off his hat, revealing the gray disordered hair*)
He will not refuse one who is so blithe to go to him.
(*Kneeling. Immediately is heard a harsh roar of kettledrums. There is total blackout at head of the stairs, while the drums roar. Then the drums cease*)

HEADSMAN (*Bangs the trap down, in the darkness*) Behold—the head—of a traitor!
(*The lights come up*)

COMMON MAN (*Comes to the center of the stage, having taken off his mask*) I'm breathing . . . Are you breathing too?
. . . It's nice, isn't it? It isn't difficult to keep alive, friends—just don't *make* trouble—or if you must make trouble, make

the sort of trouble that's expected. Well, I don't need to tell you that. Good night. If we should bump into one another, recognize me.
(*He exits*)

Curtain

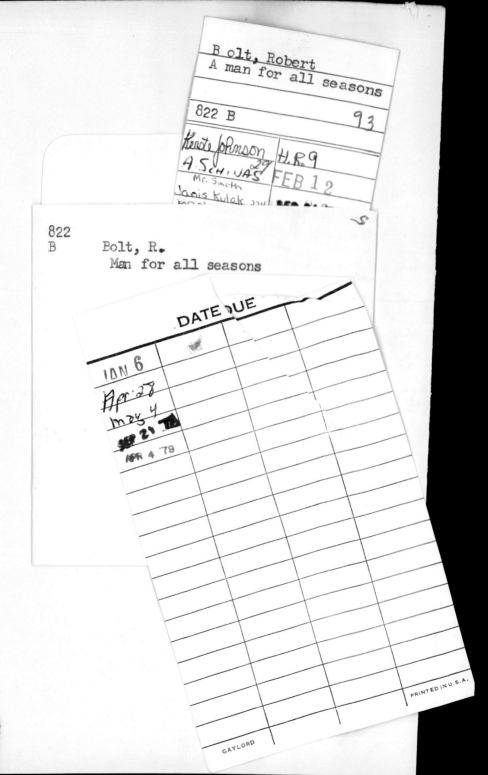

Bolt, Robert
A man for all seasons

822 B   93

Kente Johnson   H.R.9
A.SCHIVAS   FEB 12
Mr. Smith
Janis Kulak

822
B   Bolt, R.
         Man for all seasons

DATE DUE

JAN 6
Apr 28
may 4
SEP 21 78
APR 4 '79

PRINTED IN U.S.A.

GAYLORD